THE WAY OF A PILGRIM

was written by an unknown nineteenth-century Russian peasant and tells of his constant wrestling with the problem of "how to pray without ceasing." Through his journeys and travels, and under the tutelage of a spiritual father, he becomes gradually more open to the promptings of God. The reader is enriched as he shares these religious experiences in a most humble, simple, and beautiful narrative.

An extraordinary spiritual guide, THE WAY OF A PILGRIM takes its place beside these other fine Image classics:

ABANDONMENT TO DIVINE PROVIDENCE . . . ASCENT OF MT. CARMEL . . . AUTOBIOGRAPHY OF ST. THERESE OF LISIEUX . . . CITY OF GOD . . . CLOUD OF UNKNOWING . . . CONFESSIONS OF ST. AUGUSTINE . . . DARK NIGHT OF THE SOUL . . . IMITATION OF CHRIST . . . INTERIOR CASTLE . . . INTRODUCTION TO THE DEVOUT LIFE . . . LIFE OF TERESA OF JESUS . . . LITTLE FLOWERS OF ST. FRANCIS . . . LIVING FLAME OF LOVE . . . PRACTICE OF THE PRESENCE OF GOD . . . REVELATIONS OF DIVINE LOVE . . . RULE OF ST. BENEDICT . . . SOUL AFIRE . . . SPIRITUAL CANTICLE . . . SPIRITUAL EXERCISES OF ST. IGNATIUS . . . STORM OF GLORY . . . and WAY OF PERFECTION.

No Christian library should be without them.

THE WAY OF A PILGRIM

THE WAY OF A PILGRIM
and
THE PILGRIM CONTINUES HIS WAY

A NEW TRANSLATION BY
HELEN BACOVCIN

IMAGE BOOKS

A DIVISION OF DOUBLEDAY & COMPANY, INC.
GARDEN CITY, NEW YORK

Library of Congress Cataloging in Publication Data

Main entry under title:
The way of a pilgrim and The pilgrim continues his way.

Translation of Otkrovennye rasskazy strannika
dukhovnomu svoemu ottsu.
1 Spiritual life—Orthodox Eastern authors.
2. Jesus Prayer. I. Bacovcin, Helen, 1934–
BX382.O8513   248'.48'19
ISBN: 0-385-12400-7
Library of Congress Catalog Card Number 76–52000

Image Books edition published February 1978

FOREWORD

In his book *Homo Viator* Gabriel Marcel speaks of man as a pilgrim. He says in his essay "Value and Immortality," "Perhaps a stable order can only be established on earth if man always remains accurately conscious that his condition is that of a traveller." It may seem on the surface that this philosopher and the main character of *The Way of a Pilgrim*, a simple, anonymous Russian peasant who refers to himself as a pilgrim, have very little in common, that they are worlds apart in their understanding of life. But I believe that on a deeper level they are one, for they share a single vision and the source of their hope is one. They are both deeply aware that here on earth man does not have a lasting city, that his stability and security consist in being rooted in God, in that Truth which is not a thing but a person. They are both teachers: one on the theoretical level and the other on the practical. Gabriel Marcel philosophizes about man's human condition and his need of hope, while the Pilgrim shows by example, by his very life style what it means to place one's trust in God. They both know that to place one's hope in God is to have His divine light and wisdom by which to live and by which to see the world; that it is to be eminently qualified to see every man and every aspect of God's creation as it really is in the eyes of God.

The interested reader can continue with the above analogy, but I would like to take a closer look at the Pilgrim's vision of reality, and especially at the process by which he arrives at the mountain and, in the words of Kahil Gibran, "sees the beauty of the world."

The Pilgrim has climbed the mountain; he has gained profound knowledge and wisdom by means of ceaseless prayer, which he has learned under the direction of a starets, his spiritual guide, and the writings of the holy Fathers in the *Philokalia*. He was introduced to a unique form of ejaculatory prayer known as the Jesus Prayer or the Prayer of the Heart. The desert Fathers taught that this short prayer contains within itself the summary of the Gospel and that ceaseless recitation of it is a direct response to the injunction of Scripture to pray always. They regarded the Jesus Prayer as the art of arts and the science of sciences, for it could lead the man who assiduously practiced it to the heights of perfection. The Pilgrim was most receptive to this valuable knowledge about prayer, for he had been earnestly searching for a method of prayer which would satisfy his longing for uninterrupted communion with God. He spared no effort to make this simple prayer his own, and once he began to experience its beneficial effects of peace and joy, he never tired of speaking about it to anyone who would listen. His narrative is full of fascinating anecdotes as well as miraculous cures and conversions, many of which were attributed to the Jesus Prayer.

The value of the Pilgrim's story lies in its simple presentation of the power of prayer; a power which reaches far beyond the intellect and human knowledge and beyond all efforts of man seeking to find meaning in life. This power is available to all who believe in God and it can transform man's weakness, his limitations and sufferings and bring him to glory.

In this new translation Helen Bacovcin has caught the spirit of the Pilgrim, for she shares not only in his Slavic heritage but also in his love of prayer.

WALTER J. CISZEK, S.J.

PREFACE

Several years ago I received a rather significant little gift from one of my high school students, a button with the words "My God Is OK, Sorry About Yours." And while it has been comforting to believe in a God who is OK, in recent months I have had the good fortune of becoming well acquainted with a man whose God is not only OK but ABSOLUTELY WONDERFUL. This man, dear reader, is the Pilgrim who is both the author and the main character of the story which you are about to read. He is a simple Russian peasant who may have never heard of his contemporary the writer Turgenev, but he put into practice the novelist's suggestion that every man should write the story of his life.

The Pilgrim's account is both informative and entertaining and can be read on more than one level. It is touching simply as a narrative of a man whose life style is very different from yours and mine. Fortune does not smile at him, for he has lost both his material possessions and his family; he has no home of his own and a handicap prevents him from earning a living, so he wanders from one end of his vast country to another.

On the spiritual level the story is a real treasure. The Pilgrim is deeply in love with his God and never tires of communicating with Him. Through this constant communion with his Lord and Master he gains much wisdom and understanding; he learns that true riches are of the spirit and are accessible to all. He knows as few of us do that a wholehearted response to the message of the Gospel is the only one that makes sense and satisfies the very core of our being. He knows that to give God one's all means in the truest sense to gain all. He knows that the cost of discipleship will never begin to measure up to the rewards which await the faithful disciple who does the will of the Father, both here and hereafter. He knows the secret of interior freedom and what it means to have one's hunger and thirst satisfied. He knows the beauty of each creature. He knows the deep, abiding joy and peace which surpass all understanding. Yes, he knows how ABSOLUTELY WONDERFUL God is in His love and mercy to all His children but especially to those who unconditionally open their hearts to Him.

HB

THE WAY OF A PILGRIM

CHAPTER 1

By the grace of God I am a Christian, by my deeds a great sinner, and by my calling a homeless wanderer of humblest origin, roaming from place to place. My possessions consist of a knapsack with dry crusts of bread on my back and in my bosom the Holy Bible. This is all!

On the twenty-fourth Sunday after Pentecost I came to church to attend the Liturgy and entered just as the epistle was being read. The reading was from Paul's First Letter to the Thessalonians, which says in part, "Pray constantly." These words made a deep impression on me and I started thinking of how it could be possible for a man to pray without ceasing when the practical necessities of life demand so much attention. I checked my Bible and saw with my own eyes exactly what I had heard, that it is necessary to pray continuously (1 Thess. 5:17); to pray in the Spirit on every possible occasion (Eph. 6:18); in every place to lift your hands reverently in prayer (1 Tim. 2:8). I thought and thought about these words, but no understanding came to me.

What shall I do? I thought. Where can I find a person who will explain this mystery to me? I will go to the various churches where there are good preachers and perhaps I will obtain an explanation from them. And so I went. I heard many very good homilies on prayer, but they were all instructions about prayer in general: what is prayer, the necessity of prayer, and the fruits of prayer, but no one spoke of the way to succeed in prayer. I did hear a sermon on interior prayer and ceaseless prayer but nothing about attaining that form of prayer. Inasmuch as listening to public sermons had not given me any satisfaction, I stopped attending them and decided, with the grace of God, to look for an experienced and learned person who would satisfy my ardent desire and explain ceaseless prayer to me.

For a long time I traveled through various places. I read the Bible and asked for the whereabouts of a spiritual teacher or a devout and experienced director. After some time I heard of a nobleman in a certain village who takes his salvation seriously. I was told that he has a chapel in his home and does not go out but spends all his time praying and reading spiritual books. When I heard this, I ran to the mentioned village and sought out this God-fearing landowner.

"What can I do for you?" he asked me.

"I heard that you are a devout and wise man and I came, in the name of God, to ask you to explain to me the meaning of the words of St. Paul, 'Pray constantly.' How is it possible to pray continuously? I am very eager to know this and cannot in any way comprehend it."

The gentleman was silent for a moment; then he looked at me intently and said, "Ceaseless interior prayer is a continuous aspiration and a yearning of the spirit of man toward God. To succeed in this sweet exercise it is necessary to ask God frequently that He teach you to pray continuously. Pray often and fervently and prayer itself will reveal this mystery to you, how it is possible for it to be continuous, but it takes time."

Having said this, he ordered the servants to give me food; he gave me some money for the road and dismissed me. But he did not explain ceaseless prayer.

Again I went. I thought, I read, and I meditated on the words of the nobleman, but I could not understand. And my desire to understand became so intense that even my sleep was disturbed. I continued my journey for about two hundred versts[1] and then found myself in a large provincial city. I saw a monastery. At the inn where I stopped I heard that the Superior of the monastery was very kind, devout, and hospitable to strangers. I went to him. He received me warmly and offered me some refreshments.

"Reverend Father," I said, "I do not need refreshments, but I would like you to give me spiritual advice; I would like to know how to work out my salvation."

"Work out your salvation? Well, keep the commandments and pray to God and you will be saved."

"I heard that it is necessary to pray without ceasing, but I do not know how to pray without interruption and I cannot even understand what is meant by ceaseless prayer. Please explain this to me, dear Father."

"I do not know how to make this clear, dear brother. But wait, I have a book which has an explanation," and he brought a copy of St. Demetrius's *Spiritual Instructions for the Interior Man* and indicated which page I should read. I began reading the following: "The words of the Apostle, 'Pray constantly,' are to be understood as referring to mental prayer; the mind can be constantly fixed on God and communion with Him."

"Please explain to me how the mind can be always set on God, not be distracted but continuously praying."

"This is exceptionally difficult to understand unless God Himself reveals it," said the Father Superior and he did not explain.

I spent the night at the monastery and in the morning expressed my gratitude for the warm reception and continued with my journey, not knowing where it would take me. I grieved over my lack of understanding, and for consolation I read the Bible. For five days I traveled in this manner on a long and wide road, and toward the evening of the fifth day an old man caught up with me who looked like a member of some religious community.

To my question he answered that he was a monk and that his hermitage was about ten versts from the main road, and he invited me to visit the hermitage. "We receive pilgrims and strangers and give them food and lodging in our guesthouse," he said.

Since I had no inclination to stop there, I replied, "My

peace does not depend on a place to stay but on spiritual direction. I am not looking for food, as I have enough bread in my knapsack."

"And what manner of direction are you looking for; what seems to be puzzling you? Come, come dear brother, visit us; we have experienced elders[2] who can give spiritual nourishment and direct one on the path of truth according to the word of God and the writings of the holy Fathers."

"You see, Father, about a year ago while I was at a Liturgy I heard the following admonition from the Apostle Paul: 'Pray constantly.' Not being able to understand this I began to read the Bible, where in many places I found God's precept that it is necessary to pray continuously, to pray always, at all times and in all places, not only while working, not only when awake but also in one's sleep. 'I sleep but my heart is awake' (S. of S. 5:2). I was very surprised by this and could not understand how this could be possible and by what means it could be accomplished. A strong desire and curiosity took hold of me and night and day it did not leave me. For this reason I went from church to church to listen to sermons on prayer; and though I have heard very many of them, I did not receive the desired instruction, how to pray without ceasing. The homilies I heard were about the preparation for prayer or the fruits of prayer and similar things, but I did not learn how to pray without ceasing or what is the meaning of such prayer. I kept reading the Bible and in this way I tested what I had heard. But I could not find the desired knowledge, and so to this day I am left bewildered and without peace."

The elder blessed himself and began to speak: "Thank God, dear brother, for this insatiable desire to understand ceaseless mental prayer. Recognize in this a call from God and be at peace. Believe that up to this time your seeking was in accordance with God's will and you were given to understand that heavenly light regarding continuous prayer is not reached by worldly wisdom and superficial curiosity. On the contrary, it is discovered in the spirit of poverty and simplicity of heart through active experience. Therefore, it is not surprising that you did not hear about the essential act of prayer and learn how to carry it out without ceasing.

"The truth is that, though there is neither a shortage of sermons nor of treatises of various writers about prayer, for the most part these discourses are based on mental analysis and on natural considerations rather than on active experience. For this reason they teach more about the external character of prayer than the essence of prayer. One speaks beautifully about the necessity of prayer, another about its power and its benefits, and still another of the means and conditions for its accomplishment: that is, zeal, attention, warmth of heart, purity of thought, reconciliation with the enemies, humility, contrition, and so on.

"And what is prayer? And how does one learn to pray? To these primary and most fundamental questions one seldom finds an accurate explanation in the homilies of our time. These basic questions are more difficult to understand than the above-mentioned discourses and they require mystical perception in addition to academic learning. What is most unfortunate is that worldly wisdom compels these spiritual teachers to measure God's ways by human standards. Many approach prayer with a misunderstanding and think that the preparatory means and acts produce prayer. They do not see that prayer is the source of all good actions and virtue. They look upon the fruits and results of prayer as means and methods and in this way depreciate the power of prayer.

"This is contrary to Holy Scripture, because St. Paul clearly states that prayer should precede all actions: 'First of all, there should be prayers offered' (1 Tim. 2:1). The Apostle's directive indicates that the act of prayer comes first; it comes before everything else. The Christian is expected to perform many good works, but the act of prayer is fundamental because without prayer it is not possible to do good. Without frequent prayer it is not possible to find one's way to God, to understand truth, and to crucify the lusts of the flesh. Only fidelity to prayer will lead a person to enlightenment and union with Christ.

"I say frequent prayer because purity and perfection in

prayer is not within our reach, as St. Paul the Apostle indicates. The Spirit comes to help us in our weakness when we do not know how to pray (Rom. 8:26). Consequently, our only contribution toward perfection in prayer, the mother of all spiritual good, is regularity and constancy. 'If you win the mother, you will have the children also,' says St. Isaac of Syria. Acquire the habit of prayer and it will be easy for you to do good. This basic truth regarding prayer is not clearly understood or presented by those who are lacking practical experience and who are not acquainted with the mystical teachings of the holy Fathers."

The course of this conversation brought us close to the hermitage. In order not to let this wise man go, and to quickly receive my heart's desire, I hurried to ask him, "Please, be gracious, Reverend Father, and explain the meaning of ceaseless mental prayer to me and show me how I can learn to practice it. I can see that you are both well versed and experienced in this matter."

The elder received my plea lovingly and invited me to visit him in his cell: "Come, stop by and I will give you a book of the holy Fathers from which, with the help of God, you can learn all about prayer and understand it clearly and in detail." When we entered his cell, the elder said, "The ceaseless Jesus Prayer is a continuous, uninterrupted call on the holy name of Jesus Christ with the lips, mind, and heart; and in the awareness of His abiding presence it is a plea for His blessing in all undertakings, in all places, at all times, even in sleep. The words of the Prayer are: 'Lord Jesus Christ, have mercy on me!' Anyone who becomes accustomed to this Prayer will experience great comfort as well as the need to say it continuously. He will become accustomed to it to such a degree that he will not be able to do without it and eventually the Prayer will of itself flow in him.

"Now do you understand what ceaseless prayer is?" he asked me.

"Very clearly, dear Father. For the love of God please teach me how to make it my own," I exclaimed in joy.

"To learn about this prayer, we will read from a book

called the *Philokalia*.[3] This book, which was compiled by twenty-five holy Fathers, contains complete and detailed instructions about ceaseless prayer. The content of this book is of such depth and usefulness that it is considered to be the primary teacher of contemplative life, and as the Venerable Nicephorus says, 'It leads one to salvation without labor and sweat.'"

"Is it then more important than the Holy Bible?" I asked.

"No, it is neither more important nor holier than the Bible, but it contains clear exposition of the ideas that are mysteriously presented in the Bible and are not easy for our finite mind to understand. I will give you an illustration. The sun—a great, shining, and magnificent light—cannot be contemplated and looked at directly with the naked eye. An artificial glass, a million times smaller and dimmer than the sun, is needed to look at the great king of lights to be enraptured by its fiery rays. In a similar way the Holy Bible is a shining light and the *Philokalia* is the necessary glass.

"Now if you will listen, I will read how you can learn ceaseless interior prayer." The elder opened the *Philokalia* to the account of St. Simeon the New Theologian and began reading: " 'Sit alone and in silence; bow your head and close your eyes; relax your breathing and with your imagination look into your heart; direct your thoughts from your head into your heart. And while inhaling say, "Lord Jesus Christ, have mercy on me," either softly with your lips or in your mind. Endeavor to fight distractions but be patient and peaceful and repeat this process frequently.' "

The elder illustrated this passage for me and then we read the accounts of St. Gregory of Sinai and Venerable Callistus and Ignatius. All the material which we read in the *Philokalia* the elder explained in his own words. I listened with attention and delight to everything and endeavored to remember as much as I could. We spent the whole night in this way, and in the morning we went to matins[4] without having slept.

When I left, the elder blessed me and encouraged me to come to him for direction and confession during the course of my study of prayer. He said that without the guidance of a director it is not very profitable to study interior life.

Later, while standing in church I felt a burning zeal to learn ceaseless prayer and I asked God to help me in this. But then I became concerned about having a place to stay while going to the elder for direction. At the inn I could not stay more than three days and there were no apartments available close to the hermitage. Fortunately, I heard of a village about four versts away and I went there to look; God was with me and helped me to find a place. I made arrangements with a farmer to live in a little hut and guard his vegetable garden during the summer months. Praise be to God! I found a quiet place. Now I could begin to study interior prayer according to the method which was shown to me and I could still visit with the elder.

For a week I followed the instructions of the elder and studied ceaseless prayer alone in the vegetable garden, and for a while I managed. Then a great burden came upon me. Laziness, boredom, drowsiness and a cloud of disturbing thoughts seemed to overwhelm me. In my sorrow I went to see the elder and explained my situation to him.

He welcomed me lovingly and said, "Dearly beloved brother, a war has been declared against you by the world of darkness—a world which finds nothing as terrifying as heartfelt prayer and therefore tries by all means possible to confuse you and distract you from your purpose of learning how to pray. However, even the action of the enemy is permitted by God's will to the extent that it is necessary for us. It seems that your humility needs to be tested and that you are not yet ready to enter the interior of your heart, for you may fall into spiritual greediness.

"I will read you a directive from the *Philokalia* regarding such a situation." And so the elder found the instruction of the Venerable Nicephorus the Solitary and began: "'If, in spite of all effort, you cannot enter the interior of the heart in the way which was explained to you, then do what I will tell you and with God's help you will reach your goal. Man's vocal cords enable him to speak, to vocalize words. Use this ability then and, while fighting distractions, diligently and continuously say, "Lord Jesus Christ, have mercy on me!" If you will persevere for some time then, without any doubt, the path to the heart will be opened to you. This has been verified through experience.'

"Do you hear what the holy Fathers say about a case similar to yours?" asked the elder. "Therefore, you ought to receive this exhortation with faith and say the Jesus Prayer vocally as often as possible. Here is a rosary[5] on which you can count and in the beginning say the Prayer at least three thousand times a day; do not add to or take away from this number by yourself. Through this exercise God will help you to achieve the ceaseless activity of the heart."

I received this instruction joyfully, returned to my place, and began faithfully and as accurately as possible to carry out this directive of the elder. For two days it was somewhat difficult. Then it became so easy and pleasant that when I was not saying the Prayer a need arose within me to say it, and I began to say it then with much greater ease than I had experienced at the beginning.

I reported this to the elder and he suggested that I recite the Prayer six thousand times a day. He said, "Be at peace and faithfully recite the assigned number of Prayers. God will reward your effort."

For a whole week I stayed alone in my hut and recited the Jesus Prayer six thousand times every day, neither worrying about anything nor paying attention to the distracting thoughts, no matter how severe they became. My main concern was to carry out the advice of my director as accurately as possible. And do you know what happened? I became so accustomed to the Prayer that if for a short while I stopped reciting it I felt as if I were missing something, as though I had lost something. When I would begin reciting the Prayer again, I would immediately feel great joy and delight. If I happened to meet someone then, I did not feel like talking. My only desire was to be alone and to recite the Prayer. I had become so accustomed to it in a week.

As the elder had not seen me for ten days, he came to visit

me. He listened as I gave him an account of my progress and then said, "You are now accustomed to the Prayer, so continue with this good habit and strengthen it. Do not waste any time but decide, with the help of God, to recite the Prayer twelve thousand times a day. Rise earlier and retire later; stay alone, and every two weeks come to me for direction."

I did as the elder suggested, and on the first day I barely completed the assigned number by late evening. At first I felt tired in reciting the Prayer constantly; my tongue seemed numb and my jaw was tight. There was both a pleasant sensation and a slight pain in the roof of my mouth. My left thumb, with which I counted the beads, was sore, and there was an inflammation in my wrist extending to the elbow which produced a pleasant sensation. All this seemed to attract and compel me to greater accomplishment, and I spent five days faithfully reciting twelve thousand Prayers a day, experiencing both joy and longing for the Prayer.

Once, early in the morning the Prayer seemed to awaken me. I got up to read my morning prayers, but my tongue had difficulty in formulating the words and I was overwhelmed with the desire to recite the Jesus Prayer. And when I started it, it became so easy and delightful that my tongue and lips seemed to do it of themselves. I was joyful the whole day and seemingly oblivious to everything else. I seemed to be in another world, and with great ease I recited twelve thousand Prayers by early evening. I would have liked to continue but I could not go against the directions of the elder. For some days I continued in this manner, joyfully and lovingly calling on the name of Jesus.

Then I went to see the elder and told him everything in detail. He listened to me and then said, "Praise be to God that now you have both a longing for the Prayer and that the recitation of it comes easily. This is a natural result of discipline and frequent practice, which can be compared to a wheel of a machine that has been given a push and then the machine works by itself; then the wheel needs only to be oiled and nudged for the machine to keep working. Do you see with what excellent gifts the Lover of mankind has endowed even the sensual nature of man? Your own experience testifies to the kind of feelings which can be experienced, without extraordinary grace, even in impure and sinful souls. Ah, how indescribably wonderful it is when God deigns to purify a soul from passion and grants to it the gift of self-activating interior prayer. This condition is difficult to imagine and the revelation of this secret prayer is a foretaste of heavenly bliss while the soul is still here on earth. Only the simple and loving hearts who are earnestly seeking the Lord are found worthy of this! Now you may recite the Prayer as many times as you wish; call on the name of Jesus all your waking moments, without counting, and humbly resign yourself to God's will expecting help from Him. I believe that He will direct your path and will not forsake you."

After receiving this direction, I spent the rest of the summer reciting the name of Jesus vocally and I enjoyed great peace. During my sleep I often dreamed that I was praying. And if I happened to meet people during the day they all seemed as close to me as if they were my kinsmen, even though I did not know them. My thoughts had quieted down completely; I thought only of the Prayer, to which my mind now began to listen, and my heart produced certain warmth and gladness. The long Liturgy of the hermits now seemed short, and it did not tire me as in the past. My solitary hut was to me like a splendid palace, and I did not know how to thank God for sending me, a great sinner, such a holy elder for a director.

However, I was not to enjoy the guidance of my beloved and wise father for long, for at the end of the summer he passed away. With tears in my eyes I thanked him for his paternal love and teaching and said good-bye. I asked for the rosary with which he always prayed in order to have a remembrance of him. Now I was left alone. The summer had finally passed and the vegetable garden was harvested. The farmer paid me two rubles, filled my knapsack with bread, and dismissed me. Again I had no place to live, so I began to wander from place to place, but now my wandering was very different; now there was no urgency driving me. The calling on the name of Jesus Christ comforted me on the road; all people seemed good to me and I felt that everyone loved me.

One day I began thinking what I could do with the money which I had earned guarding the vegetable garden. Then it occurred to me that with the elder gone I could use a copy of the *Philokalia* so I could continue to study interior prayer. I blessed myself and continued reciting the Jesus Prayer. When I came to a provincial city, I began to inquire about the *Philokalia* in various stores. I did find the book in one store, but the price was three rubles and I had only two. I tried to make a bargain but the salesman would not change the price. In the end he said to me, "Go to that church over there and ask the sexton; he has an old copy and perhaps he will sell it to you for two rubles." So I succeeded in getting an old and battered copy and I was happy. I repaired it somehow; I sewed a cloth around the cover and placed the book in my knapsack.

So now I walk and say the Jesus Prayer without ceasing and it is more precious and sweet to me than anything else in the world. Sometimes I walk seventy or more versts a day and I do not get tired; I am only conscious of praying. When the cold air chills me, I begin saying the Prayer with greater intensity and I warm up. When hunger begins to overcome me, I begin saying the name of Jesus Christ more frequently and I forget that I wanted to eat. When I become sick and feel rheumatic pain in my back and legs, I pay greater attention to the Prayer and I do not feel the pain. When someone offends me, I remember how sweet the Jesus Prayer is and the offense and anger disappear and I forget everything. I walk in a semiconscious state without worries, interests, and temptations. My only desire and attraction is for solitude and ceaseless recitation of the Jesus Prayer. This makes me happy. God knows what this is all about. Certainly, all this is on the sensual level, or, as the late elder said, it is a natural and artificial result of habit. I am not yet ready to make the interior prayer of the heart my own, because I am ignorant and unworthy. I wait for God's good time and I trust in the prayers of my deceased spiritual father. Praise be to God that even though I have not attained the ceaseless self-activating prayer of the heart, I now clearly understand what is the meaning of the words of the Apostle Paul, "Pray constantly."

CHAPTER 2

For a long time I traveled through various places with the Jesus Prayer as my companion. The Prayer was my comfort and my courage in all my wanderings, encounters, and situations. But it occurred to me how convenient it would be to have a permanent place to stay. I would be alone and could study the *Philokalia*, which up to this time I read only when I took shelter for the night or when I rested during the day. Now I had a desire to delve into it more deeply and, with faith, to draw from it the wisdom and direction for working out my salvation by means of the prayer of the heart. However, my efforts to find a job were unsuccessful because of my handicapped left arm, which I have had since childhood, so I had to forget about having a place of my own. Instead, I decided to travel in the direction of Siberia, where I could visit the tomb of Bishop Innocent of Irkutsk. My intention was to find solitude in the Siberian woods and steppes, which would be conducive to my study and prayer.

So I set out on my journey to Siberia and I continued to recite the Jesus Prayer vocally. After some time I felt that the Prayer was somehow entering the heart by itself. The words of the Prayer seemed to be formulated according to the rhythm of the heartbeat, that is (1) Lord, (2) Jesus, (3) Christ, etc. I stopped vocalizing the Prayer and began to listen attentively as the heart spoke, and I remembered the words of my late elder in describing this joy. Then I felt a slight pain in the heart and such love toward Jesus Christ that I wished I could throw myself at His feet, lovingly embrace them, and thank Him for this great consolation which

He gives in His mercy and love to His unworthy and sinful creatures through His name.

Then I experienced a kind of blessed warmth in the heart which spread throughout my whole breast. This experience led me to a more diligent reading of the *Philokalia* to check my feelings and to learn more about the prayer of the heart. Without this test, I was afraid of falling into deception, of seeing natural acts as heavenly ones, and of giving in to pride that I had learned the Prayer so quickly. My late spiritual father had warned me of all this. So I walked more by night and I spent the days sitting under the trees in the forest and reading the *Philokalia*. Ah, how much new insight and wisdom were revealed to me in this reading! Through this practice I tasted sweetness I had not imagined up to this time. And when some of the accounts were not clear to my dull mind, the prayer of the heart enlightened my understanding, and at times I saw my late elder in my dreams and he explained many things to me, but above all he directed my unthinking soul to humility. I spent almost two summer months in such blessedness. I walked mostly through the woods and on country roads, and if I passed a village, I would stop and ask for some bread, a handful of salt, and some water, and then I would continue my journey for about a hundred versts.

Either because of my sinfulness or because I had to learn certain lessons about spiritual life, at the end of the summer there were trials in store for me. I was walking on a wide road when toward evening two men, who looked like soldiers, caught up with me and demanded money. When I tried to tell them that I did not have even a kopeck,[6] they did not believe me and impudently cried, "You are lying! Pilgrims collect a lot of money." One of the men remarked, "Why continue to speak with him," and he hit me in the head with a club so that I fell to the ground unconscious. I don't know how long I lay there unconscious, but when I came to, I saw that I was lying in the woods close to the road, all torn, and my knapsack was gone; only the cord on which I carried it was there. Praise be to God that they did not take my passport, which I kept in my old cap for convenience' sake; if the authorities asked for it I could easily get to it. I got up and began to weep bitterly, not so much because of the pain in my head as for my lost books. The Bible and the *Philokalia* were in the knapsack, and now they were gone. Day and night I could not stop my tears and sorrow as I thought, Where is the Bible which I read since I was a little boy and which I always kept close to my heart? Where is my *Philokalia*, from which I gained so much guidance and comfort? I was most unhappy without my two treasures, for I had not been sufficiently fed on them. It would have been better if they had killed me than to have left me without my spiritual nourishment. How could I ever replace those books!

For two days I could hardly move my feet, sorrow had so exhausted me, but on the third day I lost all my strength and slumped under the bushes and fell asleep. I had a dream. I was in the hermitage, in the cell of my spiritual father, grieving over my loss. The elder comforted me and said, "This is a lesson for you on detachment from material things so that your path to heaven will be more direct. This was permitted so that you would not fall into spiritual complacency. God wants a Christian to renounce completely his will, his desires, and his weaknesses and give himself up to God's will totally. He directs all happenings for the salvation of man. 'He wants everyone to be saved' (1 Tim. 2:4). 'You can trust God not to allow you to be tried beyond your strength and with any trial he will give you a way out of it and the strength to bear it' (1 Cor. 10:13). Soon your joy will far surpass your present suffering."

At these words I woke up feeling strengthened. Light and peace seemed to flood my soul. "May God's will be done," I said. I blessed myself and started on my way. The Prayer once again began to function in my heart, and I walked in peace for three days.

Then suddenly I saw on the road a group of prisoners under military escort. When I came all the way up to them, I recognized the two men who had robbed me, and as they were some distance from the others, I fell at their feet and earnestly implored them to tell me what had happened to my books. At first they did not pay any attention to me, and then one of them said, "If you will give us something, then we will tell you where they are. Give us a ruble."

I swore that I would give them a ruble without fail, even if I had to beg for it, and I offered them my passport as a pledge. They told me that the books were in the cart with the other stolen goods.

"How can I get them?" I asked.

"Ask the officer in charge of the transport."

I went to the officer and explained my situation to him in detail. Among other things he asked me, "Can you really read the Bible?"

"Not only can I read but I can write also," I answered. "You can see my name in the Bible and you can check it against my passport."

The officer then told me, "These swindlers, the runaway soldiers, lived in dugouts and robbed many people. Yesterday evening a clever coachman caught them as they were about to steal a troika[7] from him. Very likely your books are here and I will give them to you, but there is no need for you to leave the transport; you can stay with us for the night. The station is only about four versts away."

I gladly walked by the officer's riding horse and we continued with our conversation. I noticed that he was a good and honest man of middle years. He asked about my origins and destination, and I answered all his questions with complete honesty. Soon we came to the station. He found my books, gave them to me, and again invited me to spend the night with him. I accepted his invitation and stayed.

When I received my books, I was so overjoyed that I did not know how to thank God. I placed them close to my heart and held them there for so long that my hands became stiff. Tears of joy streamed down my face and my heart beat as if in ecstasy.

The officer seeing this display of affection said to me, "It is quite obvious that you love the Bible." In my joy I could not even answer him and I just continued crying. He went on,

"Dear brother, I also read the Gospel every day." With this he unbuttoned his coat and pulled out a small Kiev edition of the Gospels bound in silver. "Sit down and I will tell you what brought me to this. And let's have some supper!"

We sat down to table and the officer began his story: "I have served in the army ever since I was quite young. I knew my duties and was a favorite of my superiors as a conscientious officer. But I was young, as were also my friends, and unhappily I started drinking. It went from bad to worse until drinking became an illness. When I did not drink, I was a good officer, but when I would start drinking, then I would have to go to bed for six weeks. My superiors were patient with me for a long time, but finally, for rudeness to the commanding officer while I was drunk, they reduced my rank to private and transferred me to a garrison for three years. They threatened me with more severe punishment if I would not improve and give up drinking. In this unfortunate condition all my efforts at self-control were of no avail and I could not stay sober for any length of time. Then I heard that I was to be sent to the guardhouse and I was beside myself with anguish.

"One day I was sitting in the barracks deep in thought. A monk came in to beg alms for the church. Those who had money gave what they could. When he approached me he asked, 'Why are you so downcast?' We started talking and I told him the cause of my grief. The monk sympathized with my situation and said, 'My brother was once in a similar position, and I will tell you how he was cured. His spiritual father gave him a copy of the Gospels and strongly urged him to read a chapter whenever he wanted to take a drink. If the desire for a drink did not leave him after he read one chapter he was encouraged to read another and if necessary still another. My brother followed this advice, and after some time he lost all desire for alcoholic beverages. It is now fifteen years since he has touched a drop of alcohol. Why don't you do the same, and you will discover how beneficial the reading of the Gospels can be. I have a copy at home and will gladly bring it to you.'

"I wasn't very open to this idea so I objected, 'How can your Gospels help when neither my efforts at self-control nor medical aid could keep me sober?' I spoke in this way because I never read the Gospels.

" 'Give it a chance,' continued the monk reassuringly, 'and you will find it very helpful.'

"The next day he brought me this copy of the Gospels. I opened it, browsed through it, and said, 'I will not take it, for I cannot understand it; I am not accustomed to reading Church Slavonic.'[8]

"The monk did not give up but continued to encourage me and explained that God's special power is present in the Gospel through His words. He went on, 'At the beginning be concerned only with reading it diligently; understanding will come later. One holy man says that "even when you don't understand the word of God, the demons do, and they tremble"; and the passion for drink is without a doubt their work. And St. John Chrysostom in speaking about the power of the word of God says that the very room where the Gospel is kept has the power to ward off the spirits of darkness and thwart their intrigues.'

"I do not recall what I gave the monk when I took the copy of the Gospels from him, but I placed the book in my trunk with my other belongings and forgot about it. Some time later a strong desire to have a drink took hold of me and I opened the trunk to get some money and run to the tavern. But I saw the copy of the Gospels before I got to the money and I remembered clearly what the monk had told me. I opened the book and read the first chapter of Matthew without understanding anything. Again I remembered the monk's words, 'At the beginning be concerned only with reading it diligently; understanding will come later.' So I read another chapter and found it a bit more comprehensible. Shortly after I began reading the third chapter, the curfew bell rang and it was no longer possible for me to leave the barracks.

"In the morning my first thought was to get a drink, but then I decided to read another chapter to see what would happen. I read it and did not go. Again I wanted a drink, but I started reading and I felt better. This gave me courage, and with every temptation for a drink I began reading a chapter from the Gospels. The more I read, the easier it became, and when I finally finished reading all four Gospels the compulsion for drink had disappeared completely; I was repelled by the very thought of it. It is now twenty years since I stopped drinking alcoholic beverages.

"Everyone was surprised at the change that took place in me, and after three years I was reinstated as an officer and then climbed up the ranks until I was made a commanding officer. Later I married a fine woman; we have saved some money, which we now share with the poor. Now I have a grown son who is a fine lad and he also is an officer in the army.

"When I was cured of my drinking, I made a vow to read the Gospels every day, the account of one Evangelist in twenty-four hours; and I allow no obstacle to interfere with this practice. When duties and responsibilities are great and I am very tired when I retire at night, then I have my wife or my son read one Gospel to me and in this way I am faithful to my promise. Out of gratitude and for the glory of God I had this Gospel bound in silver and I carry it on my breast faithfully."

I was glad to hear the captain relate this story, and then I added, "I know of a similar case. In the factory of our village there was a skilled worker, a good and valuable foreman, who, unhappily, fell into the habit of drinking. Then a God-fearing man suggested that he say the Jesus Prayer thirty-three times in honor of the Blessed Trinity and the thirty-three years of Christ's earthly life. The foreman took this advice to heart, began reciting the Jesus Prayer, and soon gave up drinking completely. And what is more, within three years of this experience he entered a monastery."

"And what is more valuable, the Jesus Prayer or the Gospel?" asked the captain.

"They are equal in importance," I answered, "because the holy name of Jesus Christ contains within itself all the truths of the Gospel. The holy Fathers say that the Jesus Prayer is the abbreviated form of the Gospel."

After this conversation we prayed. The captain then read the Gospel according to St. Mark while I listened and prayed within my heart. At two o'clock in the morning we finished and went to bed.

From habit, I arose early the next morning, while all were yet asleep. And as soon as there was sufficient light, I threw myself into my beloved *Philokalia*. With what joy I opened it! It was similar to a reunion between a father and a son after a long absence, or a reunion with a friend who rose from the dead. I kissed the book, thanked God for returning it to me, and began reading the section of Theoleptus of Philadelphia in which he explains that a man can perform three distinct actions at the same time. While sitting at table, he can nourish his body, listen to spiritual reading, and pray interiorly. With great joy I remembered the previous evening, which illustrated this reading, and I realized that the mind and the heart are not the same.

When the captain got up, I went to thank him for his hospitality and to say good-bye. He gave me some tea and a ruble, and then we parted.

After walking some distance, I remembered my promise to the "soldiers," for I now unexpectedly had a ruble. For a moment there was a conflict in my mind. Should I or should I not give it to them? After all, they had beaten me and robbed me, and, since they were under arrest, they could not use the money anyway. But I also thought of what is written in the Bible, "If your enemy is hungry, you should give him food" (Rom. 12:20); and Christ Himself says, "Love your enemies" (Matt. 5:44), and "If a man takes you to law and would have your tunic, let him have your cloak as well" (Matt. 5:40). So in the end I returned to the station, and as I came close to it, I noticed that the bandits were out; they were ready to be transported to another station. I ran hurriedly toward the two men who had robbed me, gave them the ruble, and said, "Repent and pray. Jesus Christ loves you and will not abandon you." Then I left them and went on my way.

I walked for about fifty versts on a big road, and then I decided to take a country road in order to have more solitude to read the *Philokalia*. For a long time I went through the woods and only occasionally would I see a village. Sometimes I would spend the whole day in the forest conscientiously reading the *Philokalia*. I was getting knowledge and wisdom from this book and my heart was becoming kindled toward union with God by means of the interior prayer which I was learning. But at times I felt downcast that I had no permanent place where I could study peacefully and continuously.

During this time I also read the Bible, and I felt that I was beginning to understand it more clearly. In the past so much seemed incomprehensible and I was often in doubt. The holy Fathers are right in saying that the *Philokalia* is a key to the mysteries found in Holy Scripture. My earnest reading of the *Philokalia* was helping me to understand God's word. I was beginning to get an insight into such ideas as "the conversion of the heart," "real prayer," "worship in spirit and in truth," "the kingdom of God is within us," "the Spirit Himself expresses our plea in a way that could never be put into words," "abide in Me," "son give me your heart," "put on Christ," "the pledge, the Spirit, that we carry in our hearts," "the call of the heart, Abba, Father," etc.

When I began to pray with the heart, everything around me became transformed and I saw it in a new and delightful way. The trees, the grass, the earth, the air, the light, and everything seemed to be saying to me that it exists to witness to God's love for man and that it prays and sings of God's glory. Now I understood what I had read in the *Philokalia* about the "creature's knowledge of speech," and I saw how it was possible to communicate with God's creation.

For a long time I continued walking in this manner, and then I came upon such a deserted area that for three days I did not see a village. My bread was all gone and I became very hungry and fatigued. What if I die of hunger? I thought. But as soon as I began to pray with the heart, the fatigue passed. I resigned myself to the will of God and once again I was happy and at peace. Soon after, as I was passing by a very thick forest, I suddenly saw a dog running out of the woods. As I called the dog to myself and played with him for a while, I was thinking that this was indeed divine providence. Undoubtedly there were animals in these woods and this dog belonged either to a shepherd or to a hunter. I would be able to get a bit of bread somehow or, at least, ask about the nearest village. The dog frisked about me for a while and then, seeing that I had nothing to give him, ran back on the same narrow path from which he came. I followed the footpath some distance and then saw the dog in his hole barking.

From behind a large tree came a middle-aged man, emaciated and pale. He asked me how I happened to come there, and I in turn asked him what he was doing in that solitary place. And so we started a friendly conversation. The man invited me to his hut and told me that he was a woodsman guarding the forest, which had been sold to be felled. He gave me some bread and salt and we continued our conversation.

"How I envy you," I said. "You can live here in peaceful solitude, away from people, not like me roaming from place to place and jostling among all kinds of people."

"You are welcome to live here also," he said. "There is an old hut not far from here which belonged to the former woodsman, and though it is in disrepair, it is possible to live in it during the summer. As long as you have your passport, you can stay here. We will have enough bread, as I have some brought to me from the village every week, and close by we have a brook which never dries. For the past ten years, brother, I also have eaten only bread and drunk water, nothing else! But here is the situation: In the fall, when harvesting is finished, then about two hundred workmen will come to cut down this forest, and then neither you nor I can live here."

I was so happy that I did not know how to thank God for this blessing and I was ready to fall at my benefactor's feet.

What I had desired and longed for I now unexpectedly received. I would have almost four months of solitude, and I could use this quiet and peaceful time for careful reading of the *Philokalia*; I could learn more about attaining the ceaseless prayer of the heart. And so I gladly accepted the temporary lodging which was offered to me. Then I talked some more with my host and brother, and he began to tell me about his ideas on life.

"I was a respected citizen in my village," he said. "I had my own business; I dyed cotton and linen fabrics. And I was satisfied with my life, though I was not without sin; I cheated my customers, I swore and drank and quarreled. There was an old lector in our village who had a very old book about the last judgment. He would make the rounds among the orthodox Christians, and for a small donation he would read to them from this book. He visited me also. For ten kopecks he would read through the night, till cockcrow. And as I worked, I heard how the angels will blow their trumpets and God will judge the living and the dead; how the living will change and the dead will rise. I heard about the sufferings of hell; about the fire, the pitch, and the worms. Once, as I listened, I was overwhelmed with a sudden terror and I began thinking of changing my life style. Perhaps I could make up for my sins. I thought and thought and finally gave up my business, sold my house, and took this job. I only asked that the community would provide me with bread, clothes, and candles for the services.

"So this is how I have lived for more than ten years. I eat only bread and drink water once a day. Every morning I rise at cockcrow and make prostrations till dawn. When I pray, I light seven candles before the icons.[9] During the day when I guard the forest, I wear heavy chains next to my skin. I do not use abusive language, do not quarrel with anyone, do not drink beer or wine, and I have never had anything to do with women.

"At first this life style appealed to me, but lately I have been plagued with disturbing thoughts. God only knows whether it is possible to make up for one's sins, and life is full of hardship. Is what I heard from the book really true? Do people really rise from the dead? Even the dust is gone from a person who died a hundred years ago. And who knows whether there is a hell? No one has ever returned from the other world. It seems to me that, when a man dies, his body decays and he disappears without leaving a trace. And it is possible that the book was written by clerics and spiritual leaders to frighten us ignorant ones so that we would live more humbly. Life on earth is difficult; there is so little joy in it, and if there is nothing in the next world then what is it all about? Isn't it better to take life more lightly and live more happily? Thoughts like these war against me and I wonder whether I should not return to my former work."

I felt sorry for him when I heard all this and I thought, They say that only the educated and intelligent ones are freethinkers who do not believe in anything, but here one of our peasants is full of doubt and skepticism! It is easy to see that the world of darkness has access to all and perhaps even more to the uneducated ones. For this reason it is necessary, as much as possible, to acquire wisdom and to strengthen oneself with the word of God against the spiritual enemy. So, in order to help this brother and to strengthen his faith, I took the *Philokalia* out of my knapsack, opened it to chapter 109 of Venerable Hesychius, read it, and then began to explain to him that abstaining from sinful actions and fear of suffering are not sufficient for spiritual life; that only the guarding of the mind and purity of heart will free one's soul from sinful thoughts; that inner freedom can be attained only through interior prayer and, I repeated, not through fear of the sufferings of hell or even the desire for the bliss of heaven. The holy Fathers consider even heroic deeds as the acts of a hireling. They claim that the fear of suffering is the way of a slave and that desire for a reward is the way of a hireling. But God wants us to come to Him on the path of a son; motivated by love and zeal for His glory, we should conduct ourselves with honor and enjoy His saving presence in our hearts and souls.

"No matter how you drive yourself," I continued, "how

much effort you exert, and what kind of physical feats you accomplish, if you do not constantly walk in the presence of
God, with ceaseless prayer in your heart, then you will never
have peace from disturbing thoughts and you will always
have an inclination toward sin, even in small matters. I suggest, brother, that you learn how to recite the Jesus Prayer
unceasingly; it should be easy for you to do this here in solitude, and you can soon reap its benefits. You will be free
from ungodly thoughts and you will experience both faith
and love in Jesus Christ. You will know how the dead will rise
and you will truly understand how God will judge the living
and the dead. You will be surprised at the comfort and joy
the Prayer will bring into your heart; you will no longer be
bored or confused about your repentant form of life." Then
to the best of my ability, and as directed by Holy Scripture
and the writings of the holy Fathers, I taught him how to
begin and how to continue the Jesus Prayer. He seemed receptive to all this and became peaceful. So we parted and I shut
myself in the little dilapidated hut which he had shown me.

Dear Lord! What joy, peace, and consolation I experienced
the moment I crossed the threshold of that hut, which
seemed to me like a magnificent royal palace full of every
comfort and luxury. With joyful tears I thanked God for this
solitude, and thought: Now in this peace and quiet I should
apply myself conscientiously to my study and ask God for understanding. So I began to read the *Philokalia* very attentively from beginning to end. In a short time I read the whole
book and I realized what wisdom, holiness, and depth it contains. However, since the book contains so many varied
themes and exhortations, I could not understand everything.
I was unable to pull all the ideas together, particularly about
interior prayer, so that I could learn the ceaseless self-activating prayer of the heart. And this is precisely what I longed
for, as the Apostle Paul directs: "Be ambitious for the higher
gifts" (1 Cor. 12:31), and "Never try to suppress the Spirit"
(1 Thess. 5:19). I thought and thought but was incapable of
understanding this and there was no one to explain it to me.

I will implore the Lord in prayer, I thought, and He will

help me to understand it somehow. So I prayed ceaselessly for twenty-four hours, not stopping even for a little while. My thoughts quieted down and I fell asleep. I had a dream in which I saw myself in the cell of my late elder and he was explaining the *Philokalia* to me: "This book is full of wisdom; it is a secret treasure of illustrations of the hidden judgments of God. And although it is not readily available to everyone, it does contain instructions for all. It has profound sayings for the wise and simple ones for the simple-minded. You simple ones, therefore, ought not to read it in chronological order, for that order is theological. The uneducated person wishing to learn about interior prayer should read the *Philokalia* in the following order:

1. the book of Nicephorus the Solitary, in the second part;
2. the book of Gregory of Sinai with the exception of the short chapters;
3. Simeon the New Theologian about the three forms of prayer and the lesson on faith;
4. the book of Callistus and Ignatius.

The writings of these Fathers contain complete directions about interior prayer of the heart and can be easily understood by everyone.

"If, however, you desire even more simple information regarding interior prayer then find the summarized version of Patriarch Callistus of Constantinople in the fourth part of the book." I held the copy of the *Philokalia* in my hands and was looking for the mentioned section but I was slow in finding it. Then the elder himself turned a few pages and said, "Here it is! I will mark it for you," and, picking up a piece of charcoal from the floor, he made a mark in the margin where the passage was found. I listened attentively to all that the elder explained and tried to remember it.

It was still dark when I woke up, so I lay there and recalled the dream I had and what the elder had told me. I found myself thinking, God knows whether it was the soul of the elder which I saw or perhaps just my imagination since I think so much about the elder and the *Philokalia*. At dawn I got up with this perplexing question in my mind and to my astonishment I saw on the stone which served as my table the copy of the *Philokalia* opened to that very page which the elder had shown me and the section marked exactly as I saw in the dream, and even the charcoal was lying beside the book. I was completely amazed, as I remembered distinctly that the book was not there the night before; it was closed and was at the head of the bed; and I was also sure that there was no mark of any kind in that section before. This incident strengthened my faith in dreams and in the holiness of my departed spiritual father. Now I began to read the *Philokalia* in the order pointed out to me, and I read it once and then a second time. The reading enkindled in my heart a desire and zeal to experience all that I read, for now I understood clearly what interior prayer is, what means are necessary to reach it, what the results of it are, how it fills the heart and soul with joy, and how to recognize whether that joy is from God or from nature or whether it is a deception.

My first practical step was to find the place of the heart according to the directions of Simeon the New Theologian. I closed my eyes and imagined looking into my heart; my desire was to visualize the heart in the left breast and to listen attentively to its beating. At first I was occupied like this for half an hour several times a day. At the beginning I was not aware of anything but darkness; and then slowly the heart appeared and I noticed its movement. Then I began to say the Jesus Prayer interiorly to the rhythm of my breathing according to the directions of St. Gregory of Sinai and of Callistus and Ignatius: That is, while looking into the heart and inhaling I said, "Lord Jesus Christ," and while exhaling, "have mercy on me." At first I did this for an hour or two, and then I increased it so that in the end I spent practically the entire day in this exercise. When doubts or heaviness or slothfulness would come upon me, I would promptly read the section of the *Philokalia* which speaks of the activity of the heart and in this way I would renew my desire and zeal for prayer. After three weeks I began to feel pain in the heart, then a very pleasant warmth, delight, and peace. This encouraged me to even more earnest practice of the Prayer, so that all my thoughts were now directed to this and I experienced great joy. From this time, periodically, I began to experience various feelings and perceptions in my heart and mind. Sometimes I felt a sweet burning in my heart and such ease, freedom, and consolation that I seemed to be transformed and caught up in ecstasy. Sometimes I experienced a burning love toward Jesus Christ and all of God's creation. Sometimes I shed joyful tears in thanksgiving to God for His mercy to me, a great sinner. Sometimes difficult concepts became crystal clear and new ideas came to me which of myself I could not have imagined. Sometimes the warmth of the heart overflowed throughout my being and with tenderness I experienced God's presence within me. Sometimes I felt great joy in calling on the name of Jesus Christ and I realized the meaning of the words, "The kingdom of God is within you" (Luke 17:21).

These and similar consolations led me to conclude that the fruits of the prayer of the heart can be experienced in three ways: in the spirit, in the emotions, and in revelations. In the spirit one can experience the sweetness of the love of God, inner peace, purity of thought, awareness of God's presence, and ecstasy. In the emotions a pleasant warmth of the heart, a feeling of delight throughout one's being, joyful bubbling in the heart, lightness and courage, joy of life, and indifference to sickness and sorrow. And in revelation one receives the enlightenment of the mind, understanding of Holy Scripture, knowledge of speech of all creatures, renunciation of vanities, awareness of the sweetness of interior life, and confidence in the nearness of God and His love for us.

After spending almost five months in this prayerful occupation and enjoyment of the mentioned gifts, I got so accustomed to the prayer of the heart that I practiced it without ceasing and finally I felt that the Prayer of itself, without any effort on my part, began to function both in my mind and heart; it was active both day and night without the slightest interruption, regardless of what I was doing. My soul praised God and my heart overflowed with joy.

Then came the time for the forest to be cut; the workers began coming and it was necessary for me to leave my silent dwelling. I thanked the forester for his hospitality, said my prayers, kissed the spot of earth on which God made me worthy of His mercy, took the knapsack with my books, and left.

For a very long time I wandered from place to place until I reached Irkutsk. Self-activating prayer of the heart was my consolation and my joy on the entire journey; it brought me comfort in various degrees, under all circumstances, wherever I found myself or whatever I was doing. It did not distract me from anything and nothing seemed to diminish it. If I had something to do, then the Prayer flowed in me and the action was done more quickly; if I attentively listened to something or read, the Prayer did not cease and I simultaneously felt the one and the other, almost as if there were two of me or as if I had two souls in my body. My God! How mysterious man is! "Yahweh, what variety you have created, arranging everything so wisely!" (Ps. 104:24).

In my wandering I also encountered many mysterious incidents. To speak about all of them would take more than twenty-four hours but I would like to mention a few of them. One early evening in winter I was walking alone through the woods toward a town which I could already see and where I wanted to find lodging. Suddenly a big wolf came upon me and jumped at me. I had the woolen rosary which had belonged to my late elder in my hands, and in my attempt to defend myself with it the rosary slipped out of my hands and lodged around the neck of the wolf. The wolf jumped away from me and got caught in a thorny bush with his hind legs and with the rosary on a branch of a dry tree. He tried desperately to free himself but was unable to because the rosary was choking him. With faith I blessed myself and went to free the wolf and especially to get my precious rosary, for I feared that the wolf would run away with it. And, sure enough, the moment I approached the wolf and touched the rosary, he broke it and ran away without leaving a trace. I thanked God for His help in retrieving my rosary and I remembered my late elder. Then I happily reached the town and stopped at an inn to ask for lodging.

As I came inside the house, I saw two distinguished-looking men, one elderly and the other middle-aged and rather stout; they were sitting at a table in the far corner of the room drinking tea. I asked the peasant who was attending to their horses about them, and he told me that the older man was a public school teacher and the other a clerk of the district court. "Both of the men are of noble birth," he said, "and I am taking them to market about twenty versts from here." I sat there for a while and then asked the lady of the house for a needle and thread, came toward the light of the candle, and began mending my broken rosary.

The clerk looked at me and asked, "Were you making prostrations so earnestly that you even broke your rosary?"

"No, it was not I who broke it; it was a wolf," I said.

"Really? Do wolves pray?" asked the clerk, smiling.

So I gave them the details of the incident which had just occurred and also explained how valuable the rosary is to me.

The clerk again smiled and said, "You hypocrites always see miracles! What is holy in what happened? You simply flung the rosary at the wolf and he got scared and ran away. Dogs and wolves are afraid when you throw anything at them, and of course they do not wish to get caught in the woods. There is so much that is happening in the world, must we believe that everything is miraculous?"

When the teacher heard this, he joined the conversation and said to the clerk, "Don't draw such conclusions, sir! You are not familiar with this subject matter. I see in the narrative of this peasant the mystery of nature, both sensual and spiritual."

"How is that?" asked the clerk.

The teacher responded, "Though you have not been exposed to higher learning, you must have studied the history of the Old and New Testaments, published for schools in the form of questions and answers. Do you recall that, when the first man Adam was in his innocent state, all creation was subject to him and that the animals approached him with fear and he named them? The elder to whom this rosary belonged was a holy man, and holiness is nothing else than the sinner's return from his sinful state to the innocent state of the first man by means of self-discipline. When the soul of a man becomes holy, then the body is holy also. And the rosary which was constantly in the hands of the holy elder became empowered by his touch and spirit; it acquired, so to speak, the power of the first man's innocence. This is what we mean by a spiritual mystery of nature! And all animals in natural succession, even to this day, feel that power through the sense of smell, since the nose is the chief sensory organ in animals."

"You learned ones can have your wisdom and power and I take things more simply: I pour a glass of vodka and when I get it down then I will have power," said the clerk as he went toward the cupboard.

"That is your choice," said the teacher, "but leave the spiritual domain to us."

The words of the teacher pleased me and I went to him and said, "Sir, I take courage to tell you something about my elder," and I proceeded to tell him about my dream and how the elder taught me and how he marked the *Philokalia* for me.

The teacher listened attentively and the clerk who was lying on the bench cried, "It is true that from too much reading of the Bible one can lose one's wits. And that is how it is! What kind of a ghost would mark your book during the night? You simply pushed the book on the floor in your sleep and it was marred with soot. There you have a miracle! Ah, these tricksters! I have seen very much of your kind, brother." After muttering this, the clerk turned to the wall and fell asleep.

And I turned to the teacher and said, "If I may, I would like to show you the book which was marked and you can see that it was not marred with soot." I took the *Philokalia* from my knapsack, showed it to him, and commented on the awesomeness of the mystery which enables a soul without a body to pick up a piece of charcoal and write.

The teacher examined the marked page and said, "This is a

spiritual mystery and I will explain it to you. When the spirits need a physical form in which to appear before a living person, they create a visible body for themselves out of ethers and then return it to the atmosphere when they no longer need it. Because the elements of the atmosphere from which the body is made have elasticity—that is, they can expand and contract—the soul, when it is clothed with these elements, has the ability to perform different actions, including writing.

"And what kind of a book is that? May I have a look at it?" He took the *Philokalia* and opened it to the writings of Simeon the New Theologian and said, "Ah, this is a theological treatise. I have never seen it."

"Sir," I said, "this book is mostly about interior prayer of the heart; it is a detailed work of twenty-five holy Fathers on prayer in the name of Jesus Christ."

"I know something about interior prayer," said the teacher.

So I bowed to him and asked him to share with me his ideas about interior prayer.

"It is written in the New Testament that man and all creation serve vanity against their will, and that everything naturally groans and struggles to enter into the freedom of God's sons (Rom. 8:20-23). This mysterious groaning of creation and the innate aspiration of the soul is interior prayer. There is really not much one can learn about it; it is a natural quality in man."

"But how does one discover it, experience it in one's heart, and consciously practice it so that it can bring comfort and salvation?" I asked.

"I don't know whether anything is written about it in the theological tracts," answered the teacher.

"Well, here it is in this book," I said. "The subject is discussed here in great detail."

The teacher noted the title and said, "I will definitely order this book from Tobolsk and will study it carefully." Then we parted.

When I left that place, I thanked God for the fruitful discussion with the teacher and I prayed for the clerk that God would make it possible for him to read the *Philokalia* at least once and in that way lead him to salvation.

Another incident occurred in the spring. I came into one village and happened to get lodging with a priest. He was a good man and he lived alone. After I stayed with him for three days and he had a chance to get to know me a little, he said to me, "Stay with me and work for me; I need an honest and conscientious man. You see that we are in the process of building a new stone church next to the old wooden one, and I cannot find a trustworthy man who would supervise the workers and also take care of the offerings for the building. I can see that you are just the man I need and this job will be conducive to your life style. You can sit alone in the chapel and pray; there is even a special room for the watchman. Please stay at least until the church is finished." At the beginning I was quite reluctant to stay there, but the priest was so convincing that in the end I had to agree. So I stayed in the chapel through the summer, and at first I found it peaceful and conducive to prayer even though many people came to the chapel, especially on feast days. Some came to pray, others to look, and still others to steal something from the collection plate. Sometimes I would be reading the Bible or the *Philokalia* and people would talk to me or ask me to read something for them.

When I had been there for some time, I noticed a peasant girl coming to the chapel frequently and praying for long periods of time. Since her voice was audible, I realized that she was saying some strange and unorthodox prayers and I asked where she learned them. She replied that she learned them from her pious mother but that her father was a schismatic who belonged to a sect without priesthood. I was sad to hear this and suggested that she pray correctly, that is, according to the tradition of the Church. I explained the Our Father and the Hail Mary to her and also said, "Recite the Jesus Prayer frequently, for it is the most efficacious of all prayers and through it you can work out your salvation."

The girl readily accepted my advice and in all simplicity began to do what I told her. And guess what happened?

After a little while she told me that she became so accustomed to the Jesus Prayer that she had the inclination to pray continuously, that she experienced consolation and joy when she prayed, and that when she stopped she had the desire to pray again. I was happy to hear this and suggested that she continue to pray more frequently in the name of Jesus Christ.

The end of the summer was approaching. Now many of the people who visited the chapel came not only for me to read to them or to ask for advice, but they came with all kinds of human problems and even in search of lost articles. They seemed to regard me as a seer or a prophet. The already mentioned village girl also came with a problem. Her father had decided to marry her to a schismatic, by a lay person instead of a priest. "What kind of a lawful wedding is that?" she exclaimed. "It is the same as fornication. I am ready to run away and go where my eyes will lead."

I said to her, "Where will you run? They will quickly find you. It is not possible for you to hide and not be found. You had better pray to God with great fervor about this so that your father has a change of heart and will guard your soul from heresy and sin. This will be much more beneficial than running away."

As time went on, things became unbearable for me in the chapel; it was noisy and distracting. Then finally the summer ended and I decided to leave the chapel and continue with my journey as before. I approached the priest and began to explain: "You know my situation, Father. I need silence for prayer but here it is quite distracting for me. I kept my word and stayed through the summer. Now please give me your blessing for my solitary journey."

The priest was unwilling to let me go and tried to talk me out of leaving. "What interferes with your prayer here? You don't have any kind of work besides sitting in the chapel; that is an easy way to earn your bread and you can pray day and night there, brother, and really live with God! This place really needs you. When people come to the chapel, you don't speak nonsense with them, and the offerings for the church have increased. This work is more meritorious before God than your solitary prayer. What do you get from solitude? It is more joyful to pray with other people. God did not create man to be alone, to be preoccupied with himself! People should help one another and lead one another toward salvation in whatever way they can. Look at the saints and the universal teachers; they bustled and worked for the Church day and night; they preached everywhere and did not sit in solitude and did not hide from people."

"Father, everyone has his gift from God," I said. "There were many preachers but also many hermits. Each one followed his inclination and believed that God Himself was directing him on his spiritual journey. And what will you say about the saints who left their religious communities and flew to the desert for solitude so that they would not be distracted by people? St. Isaac of Syria left his bishopric for this reason, and Venerable Athanasius of Athens gave up his large monastery because these places were for them a source of temptation and because they truly believed the words of Christ, 'What, then, will a man gain if he wins the whole world and ruins his life?' " (Matt. 16:26).

"But they were saints," said the priest.

"If the saints," I answered, "were careful not to be spiritually ruined by their association with people, then what remains for the great sinner to do?"

So in the end this good priest lovingly sent me on my way.

After walking ten versts, I stopped in a village for the night. There was a desperately ill peasant at the place where I stayed, and I suggested to those attending him that they make arrangements for him to receive the Holy Eucharist. They agreed, and in the morning they sent for the village priest. I decided to stay behind to show my respect for the Holy Gifts and also to pray before this awesome mystery. I came out onto the street, sat down on a mound and waited for the priest to arrive. All of a sudden the girl who used to pray in the chapel so frequently came running to me from the back yard.

"How did you get here?" I asked.

"The day was set for my marriage to that schismatic, so I decided to run away." Then she bowed deeply to me and continued, "Please be kind and take me with you and help me get to some convent. I do not want to get married; I want to live in a convent and recite the Jesus Prayer. Some convent will accept me if you will intercede for me."

"Please," I said, "where can I take you? I do not know of even one convent in this area, and how can you come with me when you don't have a passport? I don't think that you have a chance of being accepted anywhere, and there is no place to hide at this time. They will quickly find you, return you to your home, and even punish you for vagrancy. You had better go home and pray to God, and if you don't want to get married, then feign some kind of an illness. This is called using a saving pretense, which is what Mother St. Clementa and Venerable Marina did when they took refuge in a men's monastery—as did many others."

While we sat there and talked, four men came riding a horse carriage down the road and they headed straight toward us. They took the girl, sat her in the carriage with one of the men, and sent them off; and the other three tied my hands and took me back to the village where I had spent the summer. To all my attempts to explain they only cried, "You hypocrite, we will teach you how to deceive girls!" Toward evening they brought me to the village court, put my feet in stocks, and placed me in jail until morning, when they would have the trial. When my priest friend heard that I was in jail, he came to visit me, brought me supper, comforted me, and said that as my spiritual father he would defend my character. He spent some time with me and then left.

Later that evening the district judge came through the village and stopped to visit the deputy. He was told what had happened and he decided to take care of the matter that very evening, and so they brought me to the courtroom.

We waited for a while before the judge came and with his hat still on he sat down and shouted, "Epifan! Did your daughter take anything from your house?"

"Nothing, sir."

"Is she guilty of anything indecent with this fool?"

"No, sir."

"Well then, this is what we will do: You take care of your daughter yourself, and we will give a lesson to this young man tomorrow and then release him with strict orders never to return to this village again. This is all!"

After saying this, the judge left the room and went to sleep, and I was placed in jail again. In the morning the police commissioner and his assistant came, gave me a beating, and then released me. I left the jail praising God that I was found worthy to suffer for His name. This made me happy and it intensified the prayer of the heart within me.

All that had happened seemed not to affect me; it was as if I had watched someone else being so treated. And when they flogged me, the Prayer strengthened and consoled me and I was oblivious of everything.

After I walked about four versts, I met the mother of the unwilling bride coming home from the market with her shopping. She said to me, "The groom renounced our daughter; he got mad because Akulka ran away from him." She then gave me some bread and pastry and I went on my way.

The weather was pleasant and I did not care to sleep in any village. Instead, I stopped in the woodland where I saw two stacks of hay fenced in and there I made myself comfortable for the night. When I fell asleep, I had a dream in which I was going down the road and reading the account of Anthony the Great in the *Philokalia*. All of a sudden my late elder caught up with me and said, "Don't read that but this," and he pointed to the following words in chapter 35 of John of Karpathos: "Sometimes the teacher falls into disrespect and suffers trials for those whom he helps spiritually." And then he showed me chapter 41, where it says: "Those who assiduously apply themselves to prayer are free from terrible and fierce temptations." He continued and said, "Be awake in the spirit and do not grow faint! Remember what the Apostle John said: 'You have in you one who is greater than anyone in this world' (1 John 4:4). Now you have realized that no trial is greater than man's strength. 'And with any trial he will give you a way out of it and the strength to bear it' (1 Cor. 10:13). It was this trust in God's help which strengthened the saints and led them to greater fervor in prayer. They passed their lives in ceaseless prayer not only for themselves but out of love for others. Whenever it was possible, they taught and showed this to others. Writing about this subject, St. Gregory Palamas says, 'Not only should we fulfill God's commandment to pray in the name of Jesus Christ unceasingly, but we should also show this method of prayer to everyone: to the religious, to lay people, to the wise and the simple, to men and women and children. In all without exception we should try to awaken zeal for ceaseless prayer." Venerable Callistus Telecudes writes in a similar way and says that neither the results of interior prayer, of contemplation, nor any methods of raising the soul to God should be kept for oneself alone. Rather, they should be written down for the good of all. And of course, Holy Scripture also reminds us of this responsibility: 'Brother helped by brother is a fortress, friends are like the bars of a keep' (Prov. 18:19). But under all such circumstances it is necessary to flee from vainglory and to guard oneself so that the seed of learning about God would not go to the wind."

When I awoke, my heart was full of joy and my soul full of strength and I continued with my journey. After some time another incident occurred which I would like to share with you. It was the twenty-fourth of March and I had an overwhelming desire to receive the Holy Eucharist on the following day, the feast day of the Annunciation of the Mother of God. I asked about the nearest church; and as it was about thirty versts away, I walked the rest of that day and night in order to make it in time for matins. The weather was unusually bad: It rained and snowed and it was also windy and cold. At one point it was necessary for me to cross a small brook, and as I came to the middle of it, the ice under my feet broke and I found myself in water up to my waist. And thus thoroughly wet I came for matins; I stayed for the Liturgy and received Holy Communion.

In order to spend that day in complete peace, with no interference to my spiritual joy, I asked permission from the sexton of the church to stay in the guardhouse till the next day. I spent that whole day in unspeakable joy and sweetness of heart; I lay on the plank bed of this unheated room intensely absorbed in prayer and as happy as if I were resting in the bosom of Abraham. Love for Jesus Christ and the Mother of God surged in my heart like sweet waves, and my soul was immersed in joyful ecstasy. Only during the night when I felt great aching in my legs did I remember how wet they were. I began to concentrate on the Prayer of the heart even more intensely until I lost all awareness of pain. But in the morning, when I wanted to get up, I realized that I could not move my legs; they were completely numb and stiff.

With difficulty the sexton pulled me off the bed and I sat there for two days without moving. On the third day the sexton wanted to be rid of me and said, "What trouble we will have if you die here." So, very, very slowly I pulled myself on my hands and lay on the steps of the church.

For two days I lay there, asking for help, but no one paid the least attention to me. Then finally a peasant came by who sat down next to me and began to talk. When he realized what was wrong with me he said, "What will you give me if I cure you? I suffered from the same malady and I know what medicine will cure it."

"I have nothing to give you," I answered.

"And what do you have in your knapsack?" he asked.

"Only dry bread and books."

"Then, will you work for me for at least one summer if I cure you?"

"I cannot work, for as you see, I have only one good hand and the other is almost completely withered."

"Well, is there anything you can do?" he asked.

"Nothing, really, except read and write."

"Ah, write! So then teach my son how to write. He can read a little and I would like for him to learn how to write also but a tutor's fee is twenty rubles."

So I agreed to the man's proposal and, with the help of the sexton, he brought me to his old empty barn.

He then began his curing process. In the fields, the back yards, and rubbish heaps he collected a bucketful of various kinds of putrid bones of animals and birds. He washed the bones and with a stone broke them into small pieces and placed them in a large earthen pot, which he covered with a lid that had a slit in it. Then he turned this pot upside down into another empty pot, which had been placed in a hole in the ground, and covered it completely with dirt. On top of this he arranged a pile of wood and made a fire, which burned for twenty-four hours. While adding wood to the fire, he said to me, "These bones will produce some tar." On the following day he dug up the pot from the ground with about a pint of thick, reddish, oily liquid with a strong odor as of raw meat. The formerly putrid bones were now white and transparent like mother-of-pearl. He told me to smear my legs with this liquid five times a day. And this is what happened. After twenty-four hours I felt that I could move my toes, on the third day I could bend my legs, and on the fifth day I got up and with the help of a cane I walked across the yard. In a word, within a week my legs were completely well, as before. I thanked God for this blessing and thought what great wisdom is hidden in God's creation! Dry, putrid bones, which had almost turned to dust, contain such vital power, color, and smell which brings life to a lifeless body. This is a proof of the resurrection of the body, I thought, and I would have liked to tell this to the ranger with whom I lived and perhaps in this way dispel his doubts about the resurrection.

After being healed in this way, I began to teach the youngster how to write. I used the words of the Jesus Prayer as a sample for writing and showed the boy how to join letters and form words. It was quite easy for me to teach him because during the day he worked for an estate manager and came for a lesson only when the manager slept, that is, from dawn till late morning. The boy caught on quickly and began to write in a short while.

The man for whom he worked noticed that the boy could

write and he asked him, "Who is teaching you how to write?"

The youngster replied, "A wanderer without one arm who lives in our old barn."

The manager, who was Polish, got curious and came to see me one day. He found me reading the *Philokalia* and asked, "What are you reading?"

I showed him the book and he exclaimed, "Ah, it's the *Philokalia*. When I lived in Vilna our parish priest had a copy of this book. However, I heard that the book describes tricks and strange formulas for prayer and that it was written by Greek monks; that the methods of prayer which it advocates are similar to those practiced in India and Bukhara, where the enthusiasts for prayer try to achieve a tickling of the heart by means of breathing. They foolishly consider this a natural form of prayer revealed to them by God. I think that we should pray simply and the goal of our prayer should be to pay our debts to God." Then he got up and recited the Our Father as Christ had taught. "This prayer is sufficient for the whole day," he said, "but to ceaselessly repeat the same words can drive one mad and ruin the heart."

"My dear sir, do not say such things about this holy book. It was not written by ordinary Greek monks but by the ancient holy men whom even your Church recognizes, such as Anthony the Great, Macarius the Great, St. Mark the Ascetic, St. John Chrysostom, and others. My late elder told me that the Indian and Bukharan monks took this method of interior prayer and distorted and ruined it; but all the directives about interior prayer found in the *Philokalia* have their source in the word of God. In the Holy Bible, where Christ Jesus directed us to pray the Our Father, He also commanded the prayer of the heart: 'You must love the Lord your God with all your heart, with all your soul, and with all your mind' (Matt. 22:38). 'Be on your guard, stay awake, because you never know when the time will come' (Mark 13:33). 'Make your home in me, as I make mine in you' (John 15:4). The holy Fathers also bring the testimony of King David, who says in the Psalter, 'How good Yahweh is—

only taste and see!' (Ps. 34:8), and they explain that the Christian should seek consolation and sweetness in prayer by all means possible and not merely recite the Our Father once a day. Here, I will read for you what the saints think of those who do not try to learn the habit of the prayer of the heart. They write that those who are not interested in ceaseless prayer sin in the following way: (1) they oppose the inspired word of God; (2) they do not aspire to a more perfect state of the soul but are satisfied with only the external virtue; they have no hunger and thirst for truth and therefore are deprived of the bliss and joy of God; and (3) thinking about their exterior virtue, they frequently fall into deception or pride and in this way fall away."

"You are reading something very sublime," said the manager. "How can we lay people aim to such heights?"

"Well, I will read for you even in more simple terms how good people, in very secular surroundings, learned ceaseless prayer." I opened the *Philokalia* to the writings of Simeon the New Theologian and began reading about a young man named George.

The manager was impressed and he said to me, "May I borrow this book and examine it in my free time?"

I answered, "I can give it to you only for twenty-four hours because I read it every day and I cannot be without it."

"Well at least copy out for me what you have just read and I will pay you for it."

"No payment is necessary," I said. "I will gladly do it for you if only God would grant you the gift of zeal for this Prayer." And so I promptly copied the passage which I had just read for him.

He read it to his wife and they both liked it. So from time to time they would invite me to visit them and I would read from the *Philokalia* while they drank tea and listened. One day they asked me to stay for dinner. We were eating fried fish, and the manager's wife, a kind old lady, wasn't careful and got a bone stuck in her throat. We tried our best to help her but could not, and as she was in great pain she went to bed. The manager then sent for the doctor, who was about thirty versts away, and I expressed my regrets and went home.

During the night, in light sleep, I heard the voice of my elder but I did not see anyone. The voice said to me, "Well, your host cured you and why don't you help the wife of the manager? God has commanded us to be concerned about our neighbor."

"I would gladly help, but how? I do not know of any means," I replied.

"This is what you should do: The woman has a great aversion for olive oil and she cannot tolerate even the smell of it. Therefore, give her a spoonful of olive oil to drink and this will cause her to vomit and bring up the bone. The olive oil will also soothe the wound in the throat caused by the bone and she will get well."

"But how can I give it to her if she has such an aversion for it, she won't take it," I protested.

"Ask her husband to hold her while you pour it down her throat by force."

I awoke and went quickly to the manager's house and told him what I was directed to do.

"What will your olive oil do now?" he said. "She is delirious, her throat is swollen and she is already choking. However, since olive oil is harmless let us try it." So he poured some oil into a glass and somehow we made her swallow it. She immediately began to vomit violently and brought up the bone as well as some blood; then she felt better and fell asleep.

In the morning when I went to see how she was doing, she was sitting quietly and having tea with her husband. They were marveling at the cure and especially at how I was told in a dream that she does not like olive oil, because no one besides the two of them knew about it. The doctor came and the manager's wife told him what had happened to her and I related how a peasant had cured my legs. The doctor was not surprised at all to hear about these cures and explained that in both of them natural power of healing was active. He then took out his notebook and wrote about these natural cures for future reference.

The news of this happening spread throughout the district and people began to regard me as a prophet, a doctor, and a wise man; they began coming to me with their problems from all sides. They brought me gifts and showed me respect and deference. I took this for a week and then I became afraid that distraction and vainglory would ruin my spiritual life so I left that place secretly by night.

Again I continued with my solitary journey and I experienced such great consolation that I felt as if a mountain had been removed from my shoulders. The Prayer brought me more and more joy and at times my heart burned with unspeakable love for Jesus Christ so that my whole being was caught up in ecstasy. The presence of Jesus Christ was so strongly impressed on my mind that thinking about the accounts of the Gospel seemed to bring them right before my eyes. I was touched and cried tears of joy; at times the joy was so great that I cannot begin to describe it. Sometimes for three days at a time I would not go close to a village, and in my communion with God I felt as if I were all alone in the world: one great sinner before a merciful and loving God. In solitude I found great comfort, and the sweetness in prayer was much more intense than when I was among people.

Finally I made it to Irkutsk, and after paying my respects to the relics of St. Innocent, I wondered where I would go next. I had no desire to stay in Irkutsk for any length of time because it was a very crowded city. But as I thought and walked down the street, a local merchant stopped me and asked, "Are you a stranger here? Why don't you come to my house?" And he took me to his rich house. He asked me about my background and when I told him where I came from he said, "You probably would like to go to Jerusalem; that is a holy place without compare!"

"I would gladly go," I answered, "but I have no means. I could go as far as the sea on foot but I cannot cross the sea without money."

"If you would really like to go, then I will tell you how you can," said the merchant. "Last year I sent one of our citizens from here." I fell at his feet, and he said, "Listen, I will give you a letter to take to my son, who lives in Odessa and who trades with Constantinople. He has ships and will gladly take you to Constantinople, where he will have one of his salesmen get you a place on a ship going to Jerusalem. It does not cost that much and he will pay for it."

I was filled with joy and gratitude and again fell at the feet of my great benefactor. I especially praised God for showing such fatherly love and care to a sinner who does no good to anyone, neither to himself nor others, but who like a parasite eats his bread in idleness. I spent three days with this rich merchant. He kept his promise and wrote a letter to his son about me, and so I am now on my way to Odessa with the intention of eventually reaching the holy city Jerusalem; but I am not sure it is God's will that I have the privilege of showing my respect to His life-giving grave.

CHAPTER 3

Shortly before leaving Irkutsk, I visited my spiritual father,[10] with whom I had had many talks before, and I said to him, "I am on my way to Jerusalem and have stopped by to say good-bye and to thank you for your Christlike love toward me, an unworthy wanderer."

"May God bless your journey," he said. "But you know, you have told me nothing about yourself; who you are and where you come from. I have heard a great deal about your wanderings but I would also like to know about your origins and your way of life before you began your pilgrimage."

"Fine," I said. "I will gladly tell you this brief part of my personal history also":

I was born in a village in the Orlovsky province, and after my mother and father passed away I was left with my older brother. He was ten years old and I was two, going on three. My grandfather, who was an upright and prosperous man, took us in. Grandfather owned and managed an inn on the main road of the town, and because of his kindness the house was always full of visitors. And so we lived with my grandfather. My brother was a playful lad and was always running around the town, but I stayed close by my grandfather most of the time. For the holy days grandfather would take us to church with him, and at home he often read the Bible to us; this one that I have with me here.

My brother went astray when he grew up; he began drinking. One day when I was seven years old my brother and I were resting on the hearth and he violently pushed me off and hurt my left hand. From that day my left hand has been rendered useless, as it is practically all withered.

When my grandfather realized that I was not suited for farm work, he began to make a literate boy out of me. He started to teach me how to read, and as there was no primer for me to use, he taught me from the Bible. Pointing to a phrase, he would encourage me to note the make-up of the words and to remember the letters. I still do not know how, but after some time of repeating after him, I finally learned how to read. Later, when my grandfather's sight began to fail, he would ask me to read out loud from the Bible and he would correct me. A district clerk lodged with us quite frequently and I was fascinated by his beautiful handwriting. I began to imitate him and to make words, and when he saw my interest, he gave me paper, showed me how to write, and even made quill pens for me. Thus I learned how to write. Grandfather was overjoyed at my accomplishment and spoke to me in this way: "Now that God has made it possible for you to become a real, literate man, thank Him for this blessing and pray more frequently." And so we now went to church for all the services and at home we prayed even more often. I read the "Lord Have Mercy" (Ps. 51) while grandfather and grandmother made prostrations or knelt.

When I was seventeen years old my grandmother died. Grandfather was eager for me to marry, so he said to me, "We don't have a housekeeper in the house; how can we get along without a woman? Since your older brother went astray, I would like you to get married." I was reluctant and in protest showed him my handicapped arm, but grandfather insisted and I was married to a sedate and good girl of twenty.

A year passed and grandfather became mortally ill. He called me to his side and said, "The house and the entire inheritance is yours. Live according to your conscience and do not cheat anyone. But especially pray to God, for all is from Him. Do not place your trust in anything but God. Go to church, read the Bible, and remember to pray for grandmother and me. Here is some money for you; a thousand rubles. Be careful neither to squander it nor to be stingy, and remember to give to the poor and to the church."

So my grandfather died and I buried him. My brother became envious because the entire inheritance was left to me. He was filled with rage against me, and with the enemy on his side, he even planned to kill me. So when he had the chance, he came by night while we were asleep and there were no lodgers; he broke into the room where the money was kept, took the money, and set the house on fire. By the time my wife and I realized what was happening, the fire had spread throughout the whole house and courtyard and we barely escaped with our lives. We escaped through a window in our night clothes.

We kept the Bible under our pillow, so, of course, when we escaped we took it with us. As we looked at the burning house, we said to one another, "Glory be to God! At least the Bible is saved and we have it to comfort us in our sorrow." And so we lost all our belongings in the fire, while my brother escaped without our knowledge that he was responsible for the fire. It was only later that we found this out, for while he was on a drinking binge, he bragged about stealing the money and setting fire to the estate.

Now we were poor indeed, for we were left naked and barefoot; but somehow, on credit, we built a small house and began to live as other peasants. My wife was a master of handcrafts. She took up weaving, spinning, and sewing, and she toiled day and night to support me. With my crippled hand I could not help her, so while she worked I read the Bible. Sometimes I would notice my wife crying while I read and I would ask, "Why the tears? Praise God that we are alive."

"Oh, it is not sorrow; I am touched by the wisdom of the word of God," she would say. We also remembered grandfather's admonition and we fasted often, recited the Afakist[11] to the Mother of God every morning, and in the evening made a thousand prostrations so that we would not give in to temptation. In this manner we lived peacefully for two years. What is surprising is that, though we had no knowledge and understanding of interior activity and had never heard about the Prayer of the heart, we had an attraction toward prayer. We prayed vocally and without inner awareness made bows like fools doing somersaults, and yet even long and seemingly incomprehensible prayer did not appear long or difficult but was recited with joy. Apparently what I heard from one teacher is the truth. He said that secret prayer is found within the depths of each man and that it is carried on in the soul of itself; and any man who knows how to listen hears the soul's call to outward prayer.

After two years of such quiet life my wife became seriously ill with a high fever and, after receiving the Holy Eucharist, she died on the ninth day. I was left completely alone and, of course, unable to work. Now my life was indeed difficult and it was necessary for me to become a wanderer and beg for my food. I was overwhelmed with sorrow for my wife, and when I would come into the house and notice her scarf or some other piece of her clothing, I would weep until I fell unconscious. When I could no longer bear the grief of living at home, I sold the house for twenty rubles and gave whatever clothes there were, both my wife's and mine, to the poor. Then, because of my handicap I was given a free passport, so I took my beloved Bible and set out where my eyes would lead. But as I left I wondered, Where will I go? First of all I will go to Kiev to pay my respects to the saints of God buried there and I will ask them to help me in my grief. And as soon as I made my decision I felt better and by the time I reached Kiev I was filled with joy. It has already been thirteen years, since that time, that I have been wandering through various places. I have visited many churches and monasteries but now I keep more to the plains and steppes. Now I wonder whether God will grant me the favor of reaching Jerusalem. God willing, it will be in time to bury my bones there.

"And how old are you?" asked my spiritual father.
"I am thirty-three years old."
"The age of Christ."

CHAPTER 4

Whereas my joy lies in being close to God. I have taken shelter in the Lord, continually to proclaim what you have done. (Ps. 73:28)

As I came to see my spiritual father again, I said to him, "The Russian proverb which says that man proposes and God disposes is indeed true. Today I was supposed to be on my way to the holy city Jerusalem, but as you can see I am still here. A totally unexpected incident compelled me to stay another three days in this city and I could not leave without coming to see you once again, to share with you what had happened and to ask for your advice.

"After I said good-bye to everyone, with God's help I set out on my journey and just as I was leaving the town, in the yard of the last house I passed I saw a man whom I recognized; he was once a wanderer also and I had not seen him for three years. We greeted each other and he asked me about my destination.

"I answered, 'God willing, I am on my way to Jerusalem.'

"'Praise be to God!' he exclaimed. 'I know of a good companion for you.'

"'God be with him and you,' I said, 'but don't you know that according to my custom I prefer to travel alone?'

"'Yes, I know,' he replied, 'but you will like this fellow traveler and it will be beneficial for both of you. You see, the father of the master of this house, where I work, has made a vow to go to Jerusalem and he is now getting ready to go. I think that it will be pleasant for you to travel with him. He is a resident of this town, a nice old man, and completely deaf; you either have to shout at him or write a note before he will answer. Therefore, he will not get on your nerves on the trip. He is silent most of the time even at home; and really, you could be of service to him on the trip. His son will give him a horse and a wagon to Odessa, and then these can be sold. The old man would like to go on foot, but he has luggage and some gifts for the tomb of our Lord and so a horse is a must; and your bag can be conveniently carried also. Now think, how is it possible to send a deaf old man on such a long trip? His son looked and looked for a companion for him but everyone asked for a lot of money, and it would not be safe to send him with a stranger because he will have money and other valuables with him. Brother, it would really be wonderful if you could agree to this. Do it for God's glory and out of love toward your neighbor. I will tell the master about you and he will be exceedingly happy. They are good people and have been very good to me in the two years that I have worked for them.'

"After our talk at the gate he took me into the house of his master, and when I realized that I was dealing with a very respectable family I agreed to their proposition. So now we have decided to start out on the third day of Christmas; God willing, we will leave immediately after we attend the Divine Liturgy.

"What unexpected happenings one encounters on the path of life! And always God in his divine providence is in charge of our destiny and our actions, as it is written: 'It is God, for his own loving purpose, who puts both the will and the action into you' (Phil. 2:13)."

"Dearly beloved brother, I am very happy that God so unexpectedly arranged for me to see you again for a little while," said my spiritual father. "And as you are now free, I will lovingly keep you here longer and you will tell me a bit more about the instructive encounters you have had on your long journey as a pilgrim. Your previous accounts were most interesting."

"I will gladly do this, Father," I said and I began:

A great deal of both good and bad happened to me; it is impossible to tell everything, and much of it I have already forgotten because I endeavored to remember only that which led and inspired my slothful soul to prayer. All other things I seldom thought of or rather tried to forget, being mindful of the admonition of St. Paul: "All I can say is that I forget the past and I strain ahead for what is still to come" (Phil. 3:13). My late elder used to say that obstacles to prayer come from two sides, the left and the right; that if the enemy does not succeed in turning us away from prayer by vain and sinful thoughts, then he brings to mind instructive and beautiful thoughts only to turn us away from prayer, which he cannot tolerate. And through this right-handed stealing, the soul abandons its communion with God, turns to its own thoughts, and talks to itself or to creatures. Therefore, he taught me that during prayer I should not succumb even to the most beautiful spiritual thoughts and that, if I discover at the end of the day that more time was spent in edifying thoughts and conversation than in real interior prayer of the heart, I should regard this as intemperance or spiritual greediness. This is especially true for beginners, who should spend much more time in prayer than in other acts of piety. But of course it is not good to forget everything, and some things are so deeply impressed on our minds that they are vivid even after a long period of time. Such is the memory of one devout family with which God made me worthy to spend several days.

During the time of my wanderings in the Tobolsk province I was running out of bread as I passed through a city in that district. So I stopped at one house and asked for some bread for the road.

The man of the house said to me, "Praise be to God! you have come just in time; my wife has just removed the bread from the oven and you can have a warm loaf. And please pray for us."

I thanked them and as I was putting the bread in my knapsack the lady of the house remarked, "What a poor bag you have. I will replace it for you." And she gave me a good strong bag.

I heartily thanked them again and went on. Then I stopped at a grocery store, where I asked for and received some salt in a small bag. I was happy and thanked God for my benefactors. Now I would not have to worry about food for a whole week and I could sleep in peace. Bless the Lord, O my soul! I exclaimed.

Leaving that city behind and going about five versts, from the road I noticed a poor village as well as a poor wooden church, though from the outside the church was painted and seemed in good repair. Being so close to the church, I had a desire to visit the house of God and to say a prayer there. As I came close to the church I noticed two small children playing in the meadow who were about five or six years of age. I thought that they were the priest's children for they were well dressed.

I said my prayers, and as I was walking down the road I heard someone calling, "Dear beggar, dear beggar, please wait!" I turned around and there were the two children, a boy and a girl, who had been playing in the meadow. I stopped and they came and took my hand and said, "Let's go to see mother; she loves the poor."

"I am not poor," I said; "I am just passing through the town."

"And how come you have a knapsack?" they asked.

"That contains my valuable bread," I replied.

"We must certainly go to mother, and she will give you some money for the road," they insisted.

"And where is your mother," I asked.

"There behind the church, behind that grove," they answered.

So they led me to a beautiful garden, in the midst of which

I saw a large country house. We went inside to an immaculately clean and well-furnished home.

A lady came toward us. "Welcome! Welcome! God be praised for sending you to us," she said. "Please sit down, brother." She took the knapsack from my back, placed it on the table, and motioned me to sit down in a soft, comfortable armchair. "Would you like something to eat, or would you like some tea? Is there anything I can do for you?" she asked.

"I am deeply grateful," I said, "but my bag is full of bread and I drink tea only occasionally. Your very warm welcome is more precious to me than any refreshments, and I will ask God to reward you for your Christlike love for strangers." As I said this I felt a strong desire to turn within; prayer was kindled in my heart and I needed peace and quiet in order to give full range to this self-activating flame. I needed solitude to conceal the external signs of prayer; the tears, sighs, and unusual movements of the face and lips.

Therefore I got up and said, "Please excuse me, madam, but it is time for me to go. May the Lord Jesus Christ be with you and with your beloved children."

"Oh, no! God forbid that you should leave us," she said. "I won't let you go. By evening my husband will come from the city, where he is a judge in the district court, and he will be delighted to see you. He regards every stranger as a messenger of God, and he would be disappointed indeed if he missed you. Besides, tomorrow is Sunday, so you can attend the Liturgy with us and then you can share in God's blessings to us and join us at table. On feast days we usually have about thirty poor brothers of Christ for dinner. Would you care to tell me something about yourself, and where you are going? Please, do speak with me, for I enjoy listening to spiritual conversations of the servants of God. Children, children, take the bag of the pilgrim and put it in the guest room with the icons; he will sleep there." I was so touched by her words that I wondered whether I was speaking with a real person or whether this was some kind of a vision.

And so I stayed to await the man of the house. Briefly I

told the lady about my travels and that I was on my way to
Irkutsk.

"How wonderful," she exclaimed. "You will undoubtedly
go through Tobolsk, and I have a mother there who is a nun
in the convent and who is a real ascetic. Many people go to
her for spiritual direction. We will give you a letter to take to
her as well as a book of St. John Climacus which she has
asked for and which we ordered for her from Moscow. Everything will work out just fine!"

Then it was time for dinner, so we sat down to the table
and were joined by four women. When we finished the first
course of the meal, one of the ladies got up, bowed to the
icon and then to us, and went to bring the second course;
then another lady went for the third course. I was curious
when I saw this, and I asked my hostess, "May I be bold to
ask whether these ladies are related to you?"

"Yes, they are as sisters to me," she said. "This one is the
cook, that one the wife of the coachman, this one the
housekeeper, and that one my house maid. They are all married; there are no single girls in the house."

I was edified to hear about such faithful servants of God
and again I felt an intense desire to be alone so that I could
pray. Therefore, I got up from the table and said to the lady
of the house, "You no doubt need your rest after dinner and
I would like to take a walk in the garden."

"No, I do not rest after dinner," she said, "and I will walk
with you in the garden so that you can tell me something inspiring and instructive. Otherwise the children would go after
you and they would not leave you alone for a moment, for
they really love the poor, the brothers of Christ, and pilgrims."

There was nothing I could do, so we went for a walk.
When we came into the garden, I decided to put a question
to her, thinking this would give me a greater opportunity for
silence, so I bowed to her and said, "In the name of God,
madam, will you tell me how long you have led a life of such
devotion and how did it all come about?"

"I will gladly tell you all," she replied. "You see, my

mother is the great-granddaughter of the Bishop Joasaph whose relics rest in Byelograd. My parents owned a large house in the city and they rented one wing of it to a poor nobleman and his wife. This man became ill and died, leaving his wife pregnant. Shortly afterward the woman also died, after giving birth to a baby boy. The newborn boy was a real orphan, so my mother took him in and lovingly took care of him. A year after this incident, I was born. So the boy and I grew up together, went to school together, and were as close as a brother and sister. After some time my father died also, and my mother left the city life behind and we moved to this her home town. When my adopted brother and I grew up, Mother gave us her blessing to marry and gave us this estate, while she herself entered a monastery. With her parental blessing and the inheritance she also gave us an admonition to live in a Christian manner, to pray fervently to God, and above all to keep the great commandment of loving God and neighbor, in all simplicity and humility to feed and help the poor brothers of Christ, to raise our children in the fear of God, and to treat the servants as our brothers. So this is how we have tried to live for the past ten years. We have a home for the poor and infirm in which we now have more than ten sick and handicapped people. Tomorrow we will visit them."

After this account I asked her, "Where is the book of John Climacus which you wish to send to your mother?"

"Let's go inside and I will find it for you," she said.

Just as we sat down to read it, her husband came home. When he saw me he embraced me warmly and as brothers we kissed each other. He then led me into his room as he said, "Let us go, beloved brother, into my study and you can bless my cell. I think that my wife must have gotten on your nerves. When she sees a pilgrim or a sick person, then she cannot leave him alone for a moment. This is the custom of all the members of her family."

We came into his study and I saw volumes and volumes of books, beautiful icons, and a lifesize crucifix, beneath which was the Gospel. I said a prayer and said, "Sir, this is indeed a heavenly place: You have here Christ Jesus, His immaculate Mother, and the saints, together with their books which contain their inspired words and admonitions. I think that you must often avail yourself of this heavenly treasure."

"Yes, I admit that I love to read," he said.

"What kind of books do you have here?" I asked.

"Many spiritual ones," he answered. "A whole set of the works of John Chrysostom and Basil the Great, many theological and philosophical works, as well as many sermons of modern preachers. My library is worth five thousand rubles."

"Do you have any books specifically on prayer?" I asked. "I love to read about prayer."

"Yes, I have the latest available book on prayer written by a priest from St. Petersburg," he said, and found the commentary on the Lord's Prayer, the Our Father, and we eagerly began reading it.

After some time the lady joined us; she brought us some tea, and the children brought a golden basket full of delicious pastries, such as I had never tasted before. Then my host took the book from me and gave it to his wife, saying, "We will have her read it while we refresh ourselves." So we listened as the lady read, and once again I experienced prayerful activity within my heart and the more attentively I listened to the reading the more intense the prayer became and I experienced great consolation. Suddenly in a flash I saw the image of my late elder. I roused myself, and in order to conceal what had just happened I excused myself, saying that I dozed off. I felt that my spirit was in communion with the spirit of my late father and I experienced an enlightened mind and had a great many thoughts about prayer. And just as I blessed myself to free myself from these thoughts, the lady finished reading and her husband asked me how I liked this explanation of prayer.

"I liked it very much," I answered. "The Lord's Prayer is the most valuable of all written prayers which the Christians know because the Lord Jesus Christ Himself taught it. The material we have just listened to is very good, but for the most part it deals with the active life of the Christian whereas I have read in the writings of the holy Fathers about the interior and mystical explanation of this prayer."

"Which of the Fathers write about it?" asked my host.

"Well, Maximus the Confessor and Peter Damascene in the *Philokalia* write about it," I answered.

"Will you please share with us whatever you remember?" he asked.

"Yes, gladly: The explanation which we have just heard of the phrase 'Our Father who art in heaven' reminds us of our duty to love our neighbor because we are all children of the one Father. This is very true, but the holy Fathers go a step further and say that these words invite us to raise our minds and hearts to our heavenly Father and remind us of our filial obligation to walk in God's presence from moment to moment. Again, according to your book the explanation of the words 'hallowed be thy name' is that the name of God should not be used irreverently or in unjust oaths—that the holy name of God is to be uttered reverently and never in vain; but the mystical writers see in this phrase a direct command for interior prayer of the heart. The holy name of God is to be impressed on the heart and by self-activating prayer is to make all the feelings and powers of the soul holy. In the words 'thy kingdom come' the mystical writers see a petition for inner peace, serenity, and spiritual joy in our hearts. According to your book the words 'give us this day our daily bread' are a petition for whatever is necessary for our physical life for ourselves and to help our neighbor, and Maximus the Confessor sees in these words a petition for the heavenly bread of the soul—that is, the word of God and union with Him, communion with God, and ceaseless prayer of the heart."

"Ah, such achievement is beyond mortal man's reach!" exclaimed my host. "The most a man can do, with the help of God, is to overcome slothfulness and recite the prayer vocally."

"Do not think that, sir," I replied, "for if this were beyond man's reach, then God would not command all men to do it. His strength is accomplished in weakness. And the holy Fathers, out of the abundance of their experience, suggest methods which can make this achievement easier. Of course, they recommend special means for the dedicated religious like the hermits, but for lay people also they suggest practical and realistic methods of achieving interior prayer."

"I never read anything comprehensive about this form of prayer," said my host.

"If I may, I would like to read something for you from the *Philokalia*," I said, and I opened the book to the section of Peter Damascene and began reading the following: "It is more necessary to learn to call on the name of God than it is to breathe. The Apostle Paul says that we are to pray without ceasing and by this he means that man is to remember God at all times, in all places, and under all circumstances. If you are making something, you should remember the Creator of all things; if you see light, you should remember Him who gave it to you; if you see the heavens, the earth, and sea and all that is in them, you should marvel and praise God who called them all into being; if you are clothing yourself, remember the blessings of your Creator and praise Him for being concerned about your well-being. In short, every action of every day should cause you to remember and praise God, and if you do this, then you will be praying ceaselessly and your soul will always be joyful." Then I said: "Do you see how convenient and simple this method of ceaseless prayer is and that it can be attained by anyone who has some human feelings?"

Both of my friends were impressed by this. The judge embraced me warmly, thanked me, looked at my *Philokalia* and said, "Without fail I will get a copy of that book; I will order it immediately from St. Petersburg, but for now I would like to have a copy of the article you have just read for me, so please dictate it to me." He then wrote it down quickly and beautifully and, as he did so, he exclaimed, "My God! I even have an icon of St. Damascene." He placed the writing beneath the glass of the icon and said, "Here is the living word of the servant of God, together with his picture, and it will serve as a reminder for me to put into practice his sound advice."

We then went to supper and were joined, as before, by all the people living there. There was blessed silence at table and after supper we all prayed for a long time, both the adults and the children. I was asked to read the Afakist in honor of Christ Jesus.

When the meal was over, the servants went to rest and the three of us stayed in the room. The lady brought me a white shirt and socks. I graciously thanked her and said, "I will not take the socks, madam, as I never wear them. I am accustomed to wearing leggings."

She quickly ran upstairs and brought her old caftan, of fine yellow cloth, and cut out two leggings. The judge looked at my feet and said, "Look at that poor man; his ragged footwear is falling apart," and he brought me his new overshoes. Then he said, "Come into this room; there is no one here and you can change your underwear." So I changed my clothes and returned to them.

They asked me to be seated and they began to cover my feet. I was reluctant to have them do this, but they insisted and said, "Sit down and be quiet; Christ washed the feet of His disciples." The judge wrapped the new pieces of cloth around my feet and his wife put the overshoes on. Overcome with emotion I cried and they cried with me.

Then the lady and the children went to sleep in the house and the judge and I went into the summer cottage. For a long time we did not sleep; we just lay there and talked. My host said these forceful words to me: "For God's sake and the good of your conscience will you tell me the whole truth about yourself? You may be from a noble class and are only pretending to be a simple peasant. You read, write, speak, and reason well and this cannot be the result of a peasant's upbringing."

I was astonished to hear this and said, "I told the whole and simple truth of my background both to you and to your wife; it never occurred to me to lie or deceive you. And for what? Much of what I say I heard from my beloved and wise elder or I read it in the writings of the holy Fathers. But for the most part my ignorance has been enlightened by interior prayer, which is the result of God's grace and the teachings of my late elder. What I have, every man can have. All that is necessary is to descend in silence into the depths of one's heart and call on the name of Jesus Christ frequently. In this way one can experience interior light and many things will become clear to him, even the mysteries of the kingdom of God. And what depth of mystery and what light there is when man realizes his ability to descend into himself, to see his inner self, to take pleasure in self-knowledge, to be touched and even to shed tears over his fallen and weakened will. It is not difficult to be reasonable and to speak sensibly with people, for the mind and the heart of man preceded knowledge and wisdom. When one has a mind, it is possible to cultivate it with learning and experience, but when there is no brain, no upbringing will help. The fact is that we are alienated from ourselves and have little desire really to know ourselves; we run in order to avoid meeting ourselves and we exchange truth for trinkets while we say, 'I would like to have time for prayer and the spiritual life but the cares and difficulties of this life demand all my time and energies.' And what is more important and necessary, the eternal life of the soul or the temporary life of the body about which man worries so much? It is this choice which man makes that either leads him to wisdom or keeps him in ignorance."

"Excuse my question, beloved brother, but I wasn't being just curious. Rather, feelings of respect for you and Christian understanding between us as well as an incident which occurred here two years ago prompted my question. You see, a poor old and senile man came to us with the passport of a retired soldier. He was barefooted and practically naked and spoke as little and as simply as would a peasant from the steppes. We took him into our home for the sick and poor, and, after being with us for five days, he became seriously ill. We brought him to this summer cottage and calmed him, and my wife and I tried to nurse him back to health. But his condition became worse and it was necessary to prepare him for death, so we called our parish priest to hear his confession, give him the Holy Eucharist, and anoint him. The day before he died, he got up, asked me for paper and pen, and explained that he wanted to be left alone to write his last will for his son. After his death I was to mail the will to his son at a given address in St. Petersburg. I was thoroughly amazed when I saw not only his beautiful handwriting but the style of his composition, precise in every respect and most refined. I have a copy of that will and tomorrow I will read it for you.

"My surprise and curiosity prompted me to ask the old man about his background and his life. He made me take an oath to say nothing about this before his death and then for the glory of God he told me about his past life. And here is what he said:

" 'I was a rich prince who led a very proud, luxurious, and dissipated life. My wife died and I lived with my son, who served as a captain in the Guards. Once when I was getting ready to go to a ball which was being given by a very important person, I became very angry with my valet, and, unable to control my rage, I cruelly hit him in the head and then gave orders to have him sent to the village. This took place in the evening and on the following day the valet died from inflammation of the head. The incident passed and, though I regretted my carelessness, I soon forgot about it. But after six weeks the deceased valet began to appear to me during my sleep. Every night he disturbed and reproached me with these words: "You have no conscience; you are my murderer!" Then I began to see him clearly even when I was awake. As time passed, he appeared more and more frequently until I saw him almost continuously. Then with him I began to see other spirits of the dead, peasants whom I had cruelly abused and women whom I had seduced. All of them now disturbed me to such a degree that I could neither eat nor sleep nor do anything. I lost all my strength and became so emaciated that only skin hung on my bones. All the solicitude of knowledgeable doctors brought no relief. I went abroad in search of a healing but returned after six months with no help. On the contrary the torturing visions were now even worse. I was brought back home barely alive and continued to experience, in full measure, the tortures of the suffering souls in hell, even while I was still in my body. I had no doubt now about the existence of hell or its meaning.

" 'While in this suffering condition, I realized my sins; I repented, confessed, freed all my servants, and made a vow to spend my entire life in the spirit of repentance as the lowest of the low in order to atone for my sins. When I firmly resolved to do this, my disturbing visions vanished. I experienced such great peace and joy at being reconciled with God that I cannot even begin to describe it. Now I realized what heaven is all about and how the kingdom of God is revealed in the depths of our hearts. Soon I was completely well, and so I kept my promise and left my family, carrying the passport of a retired soldier. It is now fifteen years that I have been wandering over Siberia. Sometimes I worked as a hired hand for the peasants, but regardless of what I was doing, I found my comfort in calling on the name of Jesus Christ. Ah, what bliss I tasted, what joy and peace of conscience I experienced in my renunciation. But this can be appreciated fully only by him who has suffered the tortures of hell and then has been brought to heaven by Christ, the intercessor of man.'

"After he told me all this, he gave me the will to be sent to his son, and on the following day he died. I have a copy of his will in my Bible and if you would like to read it I will get it for you."

"Please do," I said.

I opened it and read:

In the Name of the Triune and Glorious God, the Father, Son, and Holy Spirit.

My Beloved Son!

It is already fifteen years since you have seen your father, but I have nourished a paternal love for you and have inquired about your welfare from time to time. Now, before my death, my love for you prompts me to send you these few lines with the hope that they will be for you a lesson in life.

You know how I suffered because of my undisciplined and dissipated life, but you do not know how blessed I have been in experiencing the fruits of repentance.

I am dying peacefully in the house of my and your benefactor. I say your benefactor also because blessings poured on the father will touch a sensitive son. So give him some token of our gratitude.

I give you my parental blessing and I urge you to remember God and to guard your conscience. Be careful and sensible in dealing with your subordinates; be as gentle and loving as possible with them. Do not scorn the poor or strangers. Remember that it was only in poverty and wandering that your dying father found peace and solace for his suffering soul.

Calling the blessings of God upon you, I peacefully close my eyes and I hope for life eternal, through the mercy of our Lord Jesus Christ.

Your Father ———

The good judge and I continued our conversation and I asked him, "Don't you have quite a bit of trouble with your home for the sick and poor? Many of our brothers are wanderers because they have nothing to do or because they are lazy and they are thieves on the road, as I have had occasion to see."

"There are not many cases of that sort; almost all are real pilgrims," answered my host. "But when such troublemakers do come to us, we take special care of them. After living with the poor and humble brothers of Christ, they are converted and leave our home gentle and humble people. Not long ago we had such a case. One man from this area led such a corrupt life that people refused to take him in and would chase him from their gates with a stick; no one would give him even a piece of bread. He was a violent, quarrelsome drunkard and a thief. One day when he was very hungry, he came to us asking for bread and also for wine, to which he was

quite addicted. We received him warmly and said, 'You may
live with us and we will give you all the wine you want on
condition that after you have had some you will immediately
go to sleep; but if you rebel even to a small degree and wander on the streets, then we will not only throw you out and
never again take you in, but we will ask the police officer or
the governor to have you deported as a suspicious vagrant.' He
agreed to this and stayed with us. For about a week or more
he really drank a lot, as much as he wished; but because of
his addiction to the wine he kept his promise and went to
sleep or went into the garden and lay there quietly. When he
sobered up, the other brothers spoke to him kindly and encouraged him to give up drinking a little bit at a time. So he
gradually began drinking less, and finally after three months
he became an abstinent man. He has found himself a job and
no longer eats his bread in idleness. In fact, he was here
recently to thank me for my help."

What wisdom and guidance, I thought, and exclaimed,
"Blessed be God who has revealed His mercy in a home
which is under your protection!"

After this talk the judge and I fell asleep for about an hour
and a half and when we heard the church bells ringing for
matins, we got up. When we got to church, the lady of the
house was already there with the children. After matins we
took part in the Divine Liturgy. The judge, his son, and I
stood close to the altar, and the lady with her daughter stood
by the royal doors so that they could see the elevation of
the Holy Gifts. My Lord! How fervently they prayed; they
were on their knees shedding tears of joy. Their faces became so radiant that, looking at them, I also was moved to
tears.

After the Liturgy the priest, the servants, and all the poor,
about forty people altogether, went to the dining room.
There were handicapped people, sick people, and children
and they all sat around one table in silence.

I was bold enough to say gently to the judge, "In the
monasteries they read the lives of the saints during the meals;

it would be good for you to do this here, since you have many spiritual books."

The judge turned to his wife and said, "I think that is an excellent idea, Mary; let us set up a plan and it will be most edifying. I will read first and then you and then Father and then all those brothers who can read can take a turn."

The priest who sat there eating said, "I would like to listen but not to read, thank you, as I do not have free time to prepare. I come home and don't know where to turn, nothing but troubles and cares; needs of all kinds both for the children and the animals. I spend the whole day in worldly concerns and have no time to read or study. Even what I learned in the seminary I have already forgotten."

I shuddered when I heard this, but the hostess, who was sitting next to me, took my hand and said, "Father says this in all humility; he always puts himself down, but in reality he is a very devout priest and his life is one of dedicated service. He has been a widower now for twenty years and is raising a whole family of grandchildren by himself."

Hearing this, I was reminded of the saying of Nicetas Stethatos in the *Philokalia:* "The nature of things is judged by the inner attitude of the soul; that is, one infers and makes judgments from where he is. He in whom prayer and love are real does not see dichotomy in things; he does not separate the saint from the sinner and does not judge but loves all equally, as God does, who makes the sun to shine and the rain to fall on the just and unjust alike."

Again silence prevailed. Across from me sat a blind man from the home. The judge fed him; he cut his fish, gave him a spoonful at a time, and poured his soup. I found myself staring at the poor man and noticed that his mouth was continually open and his tongue was moving and quivering. I thought that he must be praying and I watched him even more intently. Toward the end of the meal one old lady became ill and began to groan. The judge and his wife took the woman to their bedroom and put her to bed; and while the wife stayed with the sick woman, the judge gave orders to have the coach readied and went for the doctor. The priest went for the Holy Eucharist, and all the people went to their places.

I felt a hunger for prayer, an intense desire for an interior outpouring because I had had no silence in forty-eight hours. My heart seemed inundated and tried to break forth its sweetness throughout my whole being. The effort of holding it in produced a great pain which, though delightful, was demanding silence and prayer. Now I realized why those in whom the self-activating prayer was real ran away from people and sought solitude. I also understood why the Venerable Isaac calls even the most spiritual and beneficial but immoderate speech empty talk and why St. Ephraim of Syria says, "Good speech is silver but silence is pure gold." Thinking in this vein, I went to the home and found that all were resting after dinner. I went to the garret, regained my peace, then rested and prayed. When the people of the house got up, I found the blind man and led him to the garden, where we sat alone and talked.

"For God's sake and the benefit of my soul, please tell me whether you are reciting the Jesus Prayer," I asked.

"Yes, I have been doing it for quite some time," he answered.

"And what do you get out of it?" I asked.

"I simply cannot be without it, both day and night," he answered.

"Beloved brother, please tell me in detail how you happened to begin this holy practice," I continued.

"You see, I am from this area, but I used to earn my living as a tailor and I traveled to the villages in various districts to make clothes for the peasants. It so happened that I stayed with a family in one village for quite a while, sewing their clothes. And one feast day, when I was not working, I noticed three books on the shelf in the icon corner and asked, 'Who reads in your family?'

" 'No one,' they replied. 'These books used to belong to our uncle, who was a literate man.'

"I took one of the books, opened it at random, and as far as I can remember I read something like this: 'Ceaseless prayer consists in constantly calling on the name of God, whether one is talking, walking, working, eating, or doing anything else; in all places and at all times it behooves us to call on the name of God.'

"After reading this passage, I began to think that this would be very convenient for me to do, and so I began whispering the prayer while I was sewing and I liked it. However, those with whom I lived in the house noticed this and made fun of me and asked, 'Are you a sorcerer or something? Why are you constantly whispering? What are you saying?' So in order not to get any notice I stopped moving my lips and said the Prayer only with my tongue. After some time I became so accustomed to it that my tongue says it of itself both day and night and I find it most comforting.

"For a long time I went about with my work like this, and then I completely lost my sight. Almost everyone in my family has suffered from glaucoma. Because of my inability to take care of myself, my community has assigned me to an almshouse in the city of Tobolsk and I will be going there shortly. These nice people want to give me a cart ride to Tobolsk."

"What was the name of the book which you were reading? Was it perhaps the *Philokalia*?" I asked.

"I really do not know; I did not even look at the front page," he answered.

"I brought out my *Philokalia*, opened it to the writings of Patriarch Callistus, and read to him the same words which he had recited from memory.

"That is exactly it," said the blind man. "Please continue reading, brother; how comforting those words are!" And when he heard the phrase "it behooves us to pray with our heart," he was eager for me to explain these words to him and asked me: "What does this mean, and how is it done?"

I proceeded to tell him that the *Philokalia* has detailed explanation about the Prayer, and he eagerly asked me to read everything to him.

"This is what we will do," I said. "When are you planning to go to Tobolsk?"

"Immediately," he answered.

"Well, tomorrow I also plan to go, and we can go together and then I can read to you all that pertains to the Prayer and I will point out to you the method of locating the place of the heart and descending into it."

"How about the cart?" he asked.

"Ah, you don't need it; it is not that far to Tobolsk, only about a hundred and fifty versts. The two of us can go slowly and it will be pleasant to walk and talk about the Prayer."

And thus we agreed. In the evening the judge himself came to call us to supper, and after supper we told him that the blind man and I would be leaving together on the following day and that there would be no need of the cart; that while walking we could more readily read the *Philokalia*.

The judge eagerly responded, "I also like the *Philokalia* very much and I have written a letter and have the money ready so that tomorrow when I go to work I can send the order to St. Petersburg and have it by return mail."

So on the following morning the two of us started out after expressing heartfelt thanks to our benefactors for their extraordinary love and kindness. The judge and his wife walked with us a verst from their home and then we parted.

So my blind friend and I walked slowly and only a little bit at a time, covering ten to fifteen versts a day, and all the remaining time we sat in quiet places and read the *Philokalia*. I read to him about the prayer of the heart in the same order which my late elder had shown to me, that is, beginning with the writings of Nicephorus the Solitary, Gregory of Sinai, etc. How avidly and attentively he listened and what great joy and comfort he found in it! But then he began to ask me questions about prayer which were beyond my ability to answer.

After I had read the appropriate sections from the *Philokalia* to him, he earnestly asked me to show him a practical method of locating the heart with the mind, introducing the name of Jesus Christ to it, and thus experiencing the joy of praying with the heart. So I began to explain it to him: "Well, even though you are blind and cannot see anything with your eyes, with your mind you can imagine and represent to yourself that which you saw before, a man, some object, or a part of your body like the hand or the foot. You can imagine any object as vividly as though you were looking at it, can't you?"

"Yes, I can," he responded.

So I continued, "Then in exactly the same way imagine your heart; direct your eyes as though you were looking at it through your breast, see the heart as vividly as you can, and listen attentively to its rhythmic beat. And when you have become accustomed to this, then begin to say the words of the Prayer, while looking into your heart, to the rhythm of your heartbeat. With the first beat say 'Lord,' with the second 'Jesus,' with the third 'Christ,' with the fourth 'have mercy,' and with the fifth 'on me.' And repeat this very frequently. This should be fairly easy for you, because you have practiced the preliminary part of the prayer of the heart. The next step, according to the writings of the Fathers, is to direct the flow of the Jesus Prayer in the heart in harmony with your breathing; that is, while inhaling say, 'Lord Jesus Christ,' and while exhaling say, 'have mercy on me.' Practice this as often as possible, gradually increasing the time, and before too long you will experience a kind of pleasant pain in the heart, a warmth, and a sense of burning. Thus, with the help of God, you will attain self-activating prayer of the heart. However, you must be extremely careful in all this to guard your imagination against any kind of visions; the holy Fathers strictly warn against this so as not to fall into deception."

My blind friend listened to all this with great attention and began fervently to do what I had suggested, especially when we stopped for the night. After five days he experienced great warmth and unspeakable joy in the heart as well as a great desire ceaselessly to say the Prayer, which led him to greater love of Jesus Christ. Sometimes he would see a light without any objects, and at other times it seemed to him that when he entered his heart a bright flame, as from a lighted candle, illumined his heart and his whole being and by this light he could see faraway objects, as the following incident illustrates.

We were going through the woods and he was silent and absorbed in prayer. Then all of a sudden he said to me, "How unfortunate! The church is burning and the tower has fallen down."

I said to him, "Stop imagining vain things; that is a temptation and you should renounce it immediately. How could you possibly see what is in the city? We are twelve versts away from it."

He listened to me and continued his prayer in silence. By evening we reached the city and I really saw some burned houses and the fallen tower, which had been built on wooden poles. A throng of spectators were around marveling that the tower did not crush anyone. After inquiring about the misfortune I realized that it took place at the same time as my blind friend was telling me about it.

He then said to me, "See, you thought that it was all my imagination, and it was real. How can I not love and praise Jesus Christ, who reveals His blessings to sinners, to the blind and ignorant! And I am grateful to you also for teaching me the prayer of the heart."

"Love Jesus Christ, and praise Him," I said, "but beware of regarding all visions as direct revelations from heaven, because they can often be the result of a natural order of things. The soul of man is not confined by matter and space; it can see both near and far and also in the dark. But we do not give this ability of the soul full scope for its activity; we suppress it either by the density of our bodies or by the confusion of our thoughts. When we clarify our thinking, when we learn how to concentrate and renounce everything in our environment which is detrimental to our spiritual life, then our soul comes to its own and begins to function on a higher, though natural level. I heard from my late elder that even people who do not pray can have this ability and that some people gain it through sickness; then in a dark room they can see light as it emanates from different objects, they can see their own image, and they can penetrate the thoughts of another. But what comes from the prayer of the heart is directly from God's grace and it is so wonderful that it is beyond all description and cannot be compared to anything material. Nothing sensual can be compared to the heavenly sweetness in the heart which comes from God's grace."

My blind friend took this to heart and became even more humble; the intensity of the prayer in his heart increased and he experienced unspeakable consolation. I was very happy about this and with my whole heart I praised God for making me worthy of knowing such a devout servant of His.

Finally we reached Tobolsk and I brought my blind friend to the almshouse, and after we parted lovingly, I continued with my journey.

For a month I walked quietly and I became deeply aware of how edifying and encouraging good examples are. I read from the *Philokalia* and checked everything which I had told my blind friend about the Prayer. His inspiring example enkindled in me fervor, gratitude, and love toward the Lord. The prayer of the heart consoled me to such a degree that I considered myself the happiest man on earth and I wondered whether the beatific vision could bring any greater consolation. Not only was I experiencing deep interior joy but I sensed a oneness with all of God's creation; people, animals, trees, and plants all seemed to have the name of Jesus Christ imprinted upon them. At times I felt such freedom of movement that it seemed I had no body which walked but I was delightfully carried through the air; at other times I descended within myself, I clearly saw all my organs and was astonished at the wisdom of the composition of the human body; at still other times I felt as happy as a king and with all these consolations I had a great desire to die and be poured out in praise and thanksgiving at the feet of Christ in the world of the spirit.

But either I took too great a delight in these consolations or perhaps God permitted me to be tried, because for some time I experienced fear and trembling in my heart. I wondered whether another misfortune was in store for me, similar to the one I had with the girl to whom I taught the Jesus Prayer. Clouds of thoughts overwhelmed me and I remembered the words of John of Carphatos that to help another spiritually one must submit to disgrace, misfortune, and temptations. So, struggling with these thoughts, I redoubled my prayer and succeeded in dispelling them as I prayed, "May God's will be done! I am ready to suffer all that Christ Jesus permits to come to me for my sinful and proud disposition." I realized that those to whom I had recently revealed the mystery of interior prayer of the heart were prepared for it by God's secret teaching even before my encounter with them. I regained my peace and continued on my way happier than before.

For two days it rained and the road was so muddy that I could hardly pull my feet out of the mud; and I walked through the steppes for fifteen versts without seeing any settlements. And then at last by evening I saw a courtyard close to the road and I thought happily, I will ask for lodging here, and tomorrow, God willing, the weather will be better.

I came into the court and saw a drunken old man in a soldier's overcoat sitting on a mound. I greeted him and asked, "Is there someone here I can ask for lodging?"

"No one but I can give you permission," shouted the man. "I am in charge here. This is a post office station and I am the postmaster."

"Then may I please spend the night here, sir?" I asked.

"And do you have a passport? Give some legal proof of your identity." I gave him the passport and while holding it in his hands he said again, "Where is your passport?"

"In your hands," I replied.

"Well, then let's go inside." The postmaster put on his eyeglasses, looked at the passport, and said, "The passport is legal and you can sleep here. I am a good man and will even give you a glass of vodka."

"I do not drink," I said.

"Well, then at least have supper with us."

So we sat down to table; the postmaster, a young cook, who also had had enough to drink, and I. During the course of the meal they abused and reproached one another and even hit one another. But finally the postmaster went to sleep in the storage room and the cook began to wash the dishes and to clean up the kitchen, but as she worked she continued to abuse the old man.

I sat there for a while and then I thought that it might take some time before she finished, so I said to her, "Where can I sleep, madam? I am very tired from the road."

"I will prepare your bed," she said, and she placed two benches together by the front window, covered them with a piece of felt, and gave me a pillow. I lay down, closed my eyes, and rested in silence.

For a long time the cook bustled about, but finally she finished, shut off the light, and came toward me. Suddenly the whole front window—the frame, glass, and splinters of wood—flew and came crashing down so that the whole house shook, and outside the window was heard painful moaning and screaming. The woman jumped to the center of the room in fright and then fell down on the floor unconscious. Utterly shocked, I jumped up, thinking that the earth had opened up under me. And then I saw two coachmen bring in a man who was covered with blood beyond recognition and my horror increased.

The man they brought in was a courier who was coming to the station for a change of horses. His coachman missed the gate and the path leading to the house and with a drawbar knocked out the window and overturned the carriage into a ditch by the house. The courier fell and cut his head on a sharp stake which supported the mound. When they brought him in, he asked for water and wine to clean his wound. Then he drank a glass of wine and shouted an order for the horses.

I was standing by him and said to him, "Sir, how can you possibly travel with such a wound?"

"The courier may never be sick," he answered and ran out.

The coachmen pulled the cook, who was unconscious, close to the stove, covered her with a blanket, and said, "She is in a state of shock, but she will come to." And the postmaster took another drink and went back to sleep.

I was left alone.

Soon the woman got up all distraught; she walked back

and forth in the house and then she went out. I said a prayer and, as I was completely exhausted, just before dawn I fell asleep.

In the morning I parted with the postmaster and went on my way. As I walked I prayed with faith, hope, and thanksgiving to the Father of all blessings, who had protected me from danger which was so close.

Six years after this incident took place, I was passing by a convent and stopped to pray in the church. After the Liturgy the Mother Superior invited me for some tea, but when some unexpected guests came, she went with them and left me with the sisters. The humble nun who poured my tea aroused my curiosity and I asked her, "Have you been in this monastery very long, sister?"

"Five years," she answered. "I was mentally disturbed when I was brought here, but God had mercy on me and healed me and then Mother Superior received me into the community and gave me the veil."

"What caused your mental disturbance?" I asked.

"Fear. I worked at a station and one night there was a terrible accident there as horses ran into the house and knocked out a window. The shock which I experienced that night caused me to lose my senses, and then for a whole year my parents took me from one holy shrine to another but it was here in this convent that I obtained a healing."

When I heard all this, I was filled with joy and I praised God, who ordains all things in wisdom.

"There were so many unusual happenings which I encountered that even three days would not suffice to tell you all," I said to my spiritual father, "but I would like to tell you just one more":

One bright summer day I was passing by a church and a cemetery which were close to the road. The church bells were ringing for the Liturgy and I decided to go. Many people from the surrounding area were also going to church, and some were sitting on the grass outside the church and, when they saw me walk briskly, said to me, "Don't be in such a hurry, for you will get tired standing in the church. The services here are very long, as our priest is sick and celebrates very slowly." And in reality the Liturgy was very long; the priest was a young man but he looked pale and worn out. He prayed very slowly and very fervently and at the end of the Liturgy he gave a simple and beautiful sermon on how to grow in the love of God.

After the Liturgy the priest invited me to his house for dinner, and as we talked, I said to him, "How slowly and devoutly you say the Liturgy, Father!"

"Yes, but my parishioners don't like it and grumble about it; yet nothing can be done, because I choose to think about every word of a prayer before I vocalize it. Prayer without interior feeling is not very effective either for the one who recites it or for the one who listens to it; everything depends on interior life and on attentive prayer! But how few people are occupied with interior activity! The reason for this is that they don't really want it; they have no yearning for spiritual life and interior enlightenment," said the priest.

"But how does one attain such depth? It seems most difficult," I said.

"It is not in the least difficult," he replied. "To be spiritually enlightened and to be an interior man one needs only to take a passage from Scripture and meditate on it; as much as possible one should hold one's attention on it and in this way one's mind will become illumined. And this is also how one should proceed in prayer; for a pure and satisfying prayer one should choose simple but powerful words and then repeat them frequently. In this way it is possible to get an appetite for prayer."

I was very pleased to hear this simple and practical but also profound explanation of prayer. Interiorly I thanked God for this devout shepherd of the Church.

After the meal the priest said to me, "You can rest awhile and I will read the word of God and prepare for tomorrow's sermon."

So, looking for a quiet place, I came into the kitchen and

saw there a very old lady sitting in the corner, bent over and coughing. I sat close to the window, took the *Philokalia* from my bag, and began to read. Soon after I sat down, I realized that the woman in the corner was reciting the Jesus Prayer without ceasing. I was very happy to hear the name of Jesus so frequently, and I turned to her and said, "How wonderful it is, dear mother, to hear you pray so constantly! This is a very Christian and meritorious act."

"Yes, may God be praised! It is such a joy in my old age," she said.

"Have you been praying like this for a long time?" I asked.

"Yes, since I was very young and now I cannot do without it; the Jesus Prayer saved me from destruction and death."

"How did that happen?" I asked. "Please tell me all about it, for the glory of God and greater appreciation of the power of the Jesus Prayer." I put the *Philokalia* in my bag, sat closer to her, and began to listen.

"When I was young and beautiful, my parents arranged a marriage for me but a misfortune intervened and changed the course of my life. The day before the wedding was to take place, the groom was on his way to our house, and before he got very far, he suddenly fell down and died. This affected and frightened me so deeply that I renounced marriage altogether and decided to live as a virgin and spend my days in prayer and in visiting the holy places. However, I could not travel alone for fear that someone would take advantage of my youth. Well, an old lady that I knew taught me the Jesus Prayer and suggested that I recite it ceaselessly on the road and in that way obtain God's protection. I took this to heart and then traveled everywhere securely, even to faraway places; my parents took care of my financial needs.

"Now that I am old and sick, the priest of this parish takes care of my needs."

I was filled with joy to hear this and I did not know how to thank God for this day on which I met such devout people. Then I asked for a blessing of the good and holy priest and joyfully went on my way.

Recently when I was passing through the Kazansky province, on my way here, I heard of yet another example of the power of the Jesus Prayer and how clearly and effectively it bears fruit even in one who seems to say it mechanically and without devotion. Once I had to spend the night in a Tartar settlement. However, when I came into the village, I saw a carriage by the window of one of the houses and a Russian coachman feeding the horses. I was glad to see this and decided to ask for lodging right there, with the hope of at least sleeping with Christians. I went up to the coachman and asked, "Where are you going?"

"I am going with my master from Kazan to Crimea," he answered.

While the coachman and I were speaking, his master opened the curtains of the carriage, looked at me, and said, "The Tartars' houses are rather uncomfortable, so I am spending the night here in the carriage."

It was a pleasant evening, and later the gentleman came out for a walk and we started talking. He asked me many questions but also told me about himself, and this is what he said: "Up to the age of sixty-five I was a captain in the navy, and then with old age I became ill with an incurable disease, the gout. When I retired from the service, I lived on my wife's farm in Crimea and was almost continuously sick. My wife was full of life and a great card player, so she found it confining and boring to live with a sick man and she left me. She went to live in Kazan with our daughter, who is married to a city official there. My wife took everything with her, even the servants; she left me with my godson, an eight-year-old boy.

"I lived in this way for three years. The boy took good care of me. He was quick and capable of doing everything around the house. He cleaned the house, made fire in the stove, cooked cereal, and got the samovar ready. But with all this he was mischievous and full of tricks. He ran around, screamed, knocked things over, and in general got on my nerves. I needed peace and quiet, for in my weariness and illness I enjoyed reading spiritual books. I had a beautiful book by Gregory Palamas on the Jesus Prayer, which I read practically all the time and I also prayed a little. The boy's conduct really disturbed me, and no threats were effective to keep him from his pranks. So this is what I decided to do with him. I made him sit down on a bench next to me and I ordered him to say the Jesus Prayer without stopping. At first he did this reluctantly and often lapsed into silence. So, to have him do exactly as I said, I had birch on hand. When he said the Prayer, I peacefully read the book or listened to how he pronounced the words, but the moment he would become silent I would show him the whip and so scared him into praying again. At last I had peace and quiet in my house! After some time I noticed that the whip was no longer necessary, for the boy recited the Prayer willingly and diligently and I noticed a change in his behavior. He became quiet and restrained and did the domestic duties with greater care. I was happy to see this and gave him more freedom.

"In the end he got so accustomed to the Prayer that he was saying it no matter what he was doing and without any coercion on my part. When I asked him what he thought of the Prayer he answered that he felt irresistibly drawn to say it constantly.

" 'What do you feel when you say it?' I asked.

" 'Nothing. I only feel good when I say it.'

" 'How, good?' I asked.

" 'I don't really know how to describe it,' he said.

" 'Do you feel happy?' I asked again.

" 'Yes, happy,' he said.

"The boy was twelve years old when the Crimean War broke out, and I took him with me to Kazan to visit my daughter. While there, he was placed in the kitchen with other people and he complained to me that the people were joking and playing among themselves and that they laughed at him and disturbed his prayer. Finally, after three months he came to me and said, 'I can't take it any longer; I am going back home. It is unbearably noisy and distracting here.'

" 'How can you go alone and so far in this cold weather?' I asked. 'Wait until I return, and then we will go together.'

"On the following day my boy disappeared. We sent people to look for him everywhere but no one could find him. At last I received a letter from Crimea, from the people that were left there on the farm, to the effect that the boy was found dead in my house on April 4, the second day of Easter. They found him lying on the floor in my room with his hands devoutly crossed over his breast, his cap under his head, and wearing the same light frock coat which he had on when I last saw him. They buried him in my garden. I was astonished to get this news, for I could not imagine how he got to the farm that fast. He left on the twenty-sixth of February and on the fourth of April he was found. At least a month is needed, and God's help, to cover the distance of three thousand versts on horses—about a hundred versts a day. And in addition to this, the boy had no warm clothes, no passport, and not even a kopeck. And if he did get a ride, then without a doubt this was an act of divine providence and God's special care for him.

"This boy," said the man, "tasted the fruit of prayer to a greater degree than I in my old age."

After this account, I said to the gentleman, "Sir, I am familiar with that beautiful book of Gregory Palamas which you enjoyed reading, but it discusses mostly the vocal Prayer of Jesus. I would suggest that you read the *Philokalia*, for in it you will find a complete explanation of how to achieve the interior prayer of the heart and mind and taste its sweet fruit." And with this I showed him my copy of the *Philokalia*. He examined the book and then promised to get himself a copy.

My God, I thought to myself, what unusual revelations of the power of God come through this Prayer! And how extraordinary and instructive is this incident: The boy was taught to pray by means of a whip and even this method resulted in great joy. Are not our cares and misfortunes the whips which God permits us to experience on our path in prayer? Why then are we confused and afraid when the hand

of our heavenly Father, full of infinite love, shows them
to us and by means of them wishes to teach us to pray fervently and thus lead us to unspeakable joy?

When I finished these accounts, I said to my spiritual father, "Please excuse me, Father, for talking so much; the
holy Fathers consider even spiritual but immoderate speech
as empty talk. It is time for me to go and find my fellow traveler to Jerusalem. Please say a prayer for me, a great sinner,
that the Lord in his infinite mercy would bless my journey
and bring good out of it."

"With my whole heart I wish you this, beloved brother,"
he replied. "May the abundant blessings of God overshadow
your path and be your companion as was the Angel Raphael
to Tobias!"

THE PILGRIM CONTINUES HIS WAY

CHAPTER 5

A year had passed since the pilgrim's last encounter with his spiritual father when, at last, a gentle knock on the door and a soft voice announced the return of this devout brother bringing great joy to the one who awaited him.

"Welcome, my beloved brother! Let us thank the Lord together for blessing your journey and bringing you back safely!"

"Glory and praise be to the Most High, the Father of all good, who in His wisdom ordains everything for the benefit of us pilgrims, strangers in an alien land! Last year I, a sinner, parted from you, and now by the grace of God I am honored to see you again and to hear your joyful greeting. And, of course, you are waiting for a detailed account of my journey to the holy city Jerusalem, where my soul so ardently longed to go and where all my energies were directed. However, sometimes matters are not within our control; we don't always get what we wish. And that is what happened to me. But I am not surprised, because how could a wretched sinner like myself be worthy of walking on the holy land where the Lord Jesus Christ left His footprints?"

You remember, Father, that I left here last year with a friend, a deaf man, and that I had a letter from a merchant in Irkutsk to his son in Odessa, who was to arrange my trip to Jerusalem. Well, we reached Odessa easily and quickly. My friend readily received a place on a ship going to Constantinople and I, with the letter, went in search of the son of the merchant from Irkutsk. I found his house without any

difficulty, but unfortunately I did not find my expected benefactor alive. He had died after a brief illness, and was buried
three weeks prior to my arrival. And though I grieved greatly
over this fact, I resigned myself to the will of God. The family, of course, was grief stricken, particularly the widow, who
was left with three small children. She was so overwhelmed
with sorrow that it seemed she would die from it. However,
even in her grief she received me warmly. Her circumstances
did not permit her to arrange my trip to Jerusalem, but she
asked me to stay there for two weeks until her father-in-law
would come to Odessa. He had promised to come to settle
the accounts of the trading business of the orphaned family.
So I stayed.

I lived there for a week, a month, and then another, but
the merchant from Irkutsk never came. Instead, he sent a letter to the effect that his circumstances would not allow him
to come and he suggested that the co-workers of his deceased
son be paid what was due to them and that the family should
come to Irkutsk as soon as possible. With their new cares of
getting ready for the trip it seemed that they were no longer
concerned about me, so I thanked them for their gracious
hospitality and left them to continue to roam throughout
Russia.

For a long time I wondered where I should go and then
finally I decided to go to Kiev, where I had not been for
many years.

At the beginning I most certainly grieved that my desire to
be in Jerusalem was not fulfilled, but I realized that divine
providence had directed this and I comforted myself with the
hope that the Lord, the Lover of mankind, would accept my
intention as an act and would not leave my wretched journey
without some spiritual benefit.

And in reality this is what happened, for I met people who
informed me about things which I did not know, and in this
way guided my poor soul to salvation. If necessity had not
directed me on this journey, then I would not have met my
spiritual benefactors.

As I traveled, the Prayer was my companion by day, and at

night when I took lodging I read the *Philokalia* for the strengthening and inspiration of my soul in its struggle with the unseen enemies of salvation.

When I was about seventy versts away from Odessa, I witnessed a very strange incident. I caught up with a long train, consisting of about thirty wagons, transporting merchandise. The man in charge of the transport walked by his horse at the head of the train, and the rest of the men were in a group some distance behind. They were passing by a stream which was full of broken ice, churning and making a great deal of noise, when suddenly the young leader stopped his horse, which made the whole train stop, and he began to undress. When the drivers who were behind came to him and asked him what he was doing, he responded that he had a great desire to swim in the stream. The men were completely amazed and some laughed at him. Others called him mad and tried to prevent him from undressing, while his older brother pushed him and tried to make him go on leading the train. But no one could influence him.

Then for fun some of the younger drivers filled the horses' buckets with water and began to throw it at him as they shouted, "Here is your chance to swim."

But the moment the water touched him, the young man exclaimed, "How wonderful," and he sat down on the ground.

The men continued to splash water at him and in a short while he lay down and died peacefully. The men became frightened and utterly confused why such a thing happened. The older ones said that it should be reported to the authorities, and the others concluded that this was simply the man's fate, that such a death was assigned to him.

I stood around them for about an hour and then I went on my way. After walking about five versts, I saw a village close to a high road and I went there. I met an old priest walking down the street and I was anxious to tell him what I had just witnessed and get his opinion on it. The priest invited me to his house and I related to him what I had seen and asked him to explain to me the reason for such an occurrence.

"I do not know exactly what to tell you, beloved brother, except that there is much that is mysterious and incomprehensible in nature. I think that God premits this to happen so that man will see more clearly how divine providence rules all nature, including changes in its laws. I myself once witnessed a similar occurrence. Not far from our village there is a deep ravine, not very wide but about seventy feet deep; it is frightening even to look at its dark bottom. There is a small bridge built over it for pedestrians. A peasant from my parish, a family man of good reputation, for no reason at all suddenly had an irresistible desire to throw himself down from that little bridge into the abyss. For a whole week he struggled with this unnatural yearning and, not being able to overcome it, he got up early one morning, went to the bridge, and threw himself down. Soon some people passing by heard his moaning, and with great difficulty they brought him up, with both of his legs broken. When they asked him how he happened to fall, he replied that even though he was now in great pain, he was at peace, for he had fulfilled the irresistible desire which had caused him such mental anguish that he was ready to die only to have it satisfied.

"For more than a year he received medical care in a city hospital, and I visited him often. Like you, I was curious and I asked the doctors what they thought was the cause of such a strange action. Practically all the doctors said that it was temporary madness. When I asked them for a scientific explanation and how this madness happens to come upon an individual, I was told that it is a mystery of nature and that science has not yet discovered its cause. And I commented that if in this particular mystery of nature man would turn to God with earnest prayer and confess this to a good and wise person, that temporary madness would not win out. Though, indeed, there are many experiences in life for which there is no clear explanation."

It became dark as we talked, so I stayed for the night. In the morning the district police officer sent a clerk to ask the priest for permission to bury the dead man in the cemetery because the doctor who performed the autopsy found no signs of insanity and attributed the death of the young man to a stroke.

"See," the priest said to me, "even the medical field could not find a reason for his uncontrollable urge for water."

Then I parted with the priest and continued on my journey.

I traveled for several days and was rather tired when I came to a fairly large commercial city called Byelaya Tserkov, and as it was already evening, I began to look for a place to spend the night. In the market place I met a man who also looked like a traveler and who was making inquiries in the stores about the location of a particular resident.

When he saw me, he said, "It is obvious that you are a stranger here also, so let's go together and find a man named Yevrejnov. He is a good Christian who owns an inn and likes to receive pilgrims. I even have a note to that effect."

I gladly agreed and we quickly found his house. We did not find the man of the house at home, but his wife, a good old woman, received us graciously and showed us to a private room in the garret where we could rest. We made ourselves comfortable and rested awhile and when the owner came home we were called to supper. At supper we asked one another where each was from and somehow came to the subject of our host's last name and why he is called Yevrejnov.[12]

"I will tell you a remarkable incident concerning this," he said, and began to recount this story: "You see, my father was a Jew. He was born in the city of Schlov, and he was very hostile toward Christians. While he was still quite young, he wanted to be a rabbi and began to study in preparation for this position. He listened diligently to all the Jewish tales which could be used to refute Christianity. One day he was passing through a Christian cemetery and saw a human skull with some very disfigured teeth, which must have come from a recent grave. In his bitterness toward Christians he began to make fun of this skull; he spat on it, cursed it, and trampled on it with his feet. Then he picked it up with a stick and made a scarecrow with it. After satisfying himself in this way, he went on to his destination.

"On the following night as soon as he fell asleep he had a vision of a stranger who forcefully reproached him, saying, 'How could you have outraged my perishable remains so cruelly? I am a Christian and you are an enemy of Christ!' Several times each night this vision was repeated and disturbed both his peace and his sleep. Then he began to see the vision before him even during the day and also to hear the reproaching voice. It got progressively worse and became so frequent that my father became exhausted, terrified, and completely despondent.

"He went to his rabbi, who prayed over him and exorcised him, but the vision did not disappear; on the contrary, it got worse. When the rumor of this occurrence had spread, an acquaintance of his, a Christian whom he knew through trade, suggested that my father become a Christian to get rid of this disturbing vision, since nothing else would help. And though my Jewish father did not much like this suggestion, he said, 'I will gladly do it if only I can be free of this torturous and unbearable vision.' The Christian was happy to hear this and suggested further that my father send a petition to the local bishop asking for baptism and to be received as a member of the Christian Church. They wrote out the petition and my Jewish father reluctantly signed it. And a wondrous thing happened! From the moment that he signed the petition the vision disappeared, never to return.

"My father was completely at peace and very happy. He experienced such great faith in Jesus Christ that he visited the bishop without delay, explained the whole thing to him, and asked to be baptized. He learned the teachings of the Church eagerly and quickly and was baptized. Then he came to live to this area, married my mother, a good Christian woman, and led a prosperous and exemplary life. He was very generous to the poor and encouraged me to be the same. Before he died, he blessed me and commanded me to share with the poor. So here you have it! This is why they call me Yevrejnov!"

I listened to this account with respect and feeling and thought to myself, My God! How merciful is our Lord Jesus

Christ and how great is His love! By what different paths He draws sinners to Himself and with what wisdom He transforms small happenings into great and significant ones! Who could have foreseen that the misconduct of the Jew over the dead bones would lead him to the knowledge of Jesus Christ and to a devout life?

After supper we thanked God and our host and went to our room to rest. Since neither one of us was sleepy, we talked. My companion told me that he was a merchant of Mogilev and that he had lived as a novice in a monastery in Bessarabia for two years with a temporary passport. Now he was on his way home so that he could get permission from the merchants' society to enter the monastery permanently. He spoke highly of the monasteries in Bessarabia for their regulations, order, and the disciplined life of many pious elders living there, and he assured me that comparing the monasteries of Bessarabia with the Russian ones was like comparing heaven and earth. He encouraged me to go there also.

While we were talking about these things, a third guest came in who was a noncommissioned officer on leave from the service of the army. We noticed that he was very tired from the road, so we said our prayers and went to sleep. In the morning just as we were getting ready for the road and wanted to stop to thank our host, the matins bells rang. The merchant and I both wanted to go to church, for we knew that our trip would then be more enjoyable, so we decided to go and even asked the officer to join us.

But he replied, "What is the point of going to church when we should be traveling, and what gain does God have if we do go? When we get home we can say our prayers! You two may go if you like but I will not go. While you are at matins I will walk five versts and I am in a hurry to get home."

To this the merchant said, "Look, brother, don't predict how God will arrange things!"

So the merchant and I went to church and the officer headed for the road. After matins we stayed for the Liturgy also, and then we returned to our room and were getting our bags ready when we noticed that the housekeeper was bringing the samovar.

"Where are you going?" she asked. "You must first have dinner and some tea. We will not let you go hungry." So we stayed and in less than half an hour, while we were still drinking tea, the officer came running, all out of breath.

"I return both happy and sad," he said.

"What happened?" we asked.

"I will tell you! When I left here I decided to stop at a tavern to get some change as well as have a drink of vodka so that it would be easier for me to walk. I did this, I got my change, and then flew for the road like a falcon. After I walked about three versts I decided to count my money to see whether I had all of it. I sat down, took out my wallet, counted the money, and found it all there, but I discovered to my great horror that my passport was gone; I could not find it among my papers and the money. I got so upset that I almost lost my head. But then it occurred to me that I probably had dropped it in the tavern while I was getting change. I must run back, I thought. So I ran and ran but I was filled with doubt: What if it is not there? What trouble I will have! When I returned to the tavern and asked the attendant about it, he replied: 'I have not seen it,' and again I was filled with dread. I began looking carefully in the places where I had stood and walked about. And guess what? I was very lucky, for I found it, still folded, where it had fallen on the floor, trampled underfoot among straw and dirt. Glory be to God! I was so happy that I felt as if a big burden fell off my shoulders! The passport is soiled and in such a battered condition that I could be clobbered for it; still, without too much trouble I will be able to get home and then back to the army with it. I came back to tell you what had happened and also to ask for some ointment for my foot. With so much running I rubbed my foot till it is raw, and I can hardly walk."

"So that is what happened, brother! No doubt this happened because you refused to come to church with us to pray before beginning your journey," said the merchant. "You wanted to be ahead of us but you came back, and disabled at that. I warned you about your prediction, and you see how things turned out.

"It was a small thing that you did not want to go to church but you had to add, 'Of what profit is it to God if we pray?' This is not the way to look at things, brother. Of course God does not need prayer from us sinners, but in His love for us He likes to see us pray. Not only is the highest form of prayer, which the Holy Spirit initiates and arouses in us, pleasing to Him—a prayer which He commands us to carry out in the words 'Abide in me and I in you'; but even small acts done in His name are pleasing in His sight—every thought and intention directed to His glory and our salvation. And in His boundless mercy God richly rewards us for all this. God, in His love, rewards man a thousand times more than his actions deserve. If you will give God a mite, then He will give you a gold piece. If you will only decide to go to your Father, He will come to meet you. When you feebly say, 'Lord receive me and have mercy on me!' He embraces you and kisses you. This is the kind of love that the heavenly Father has for us unworthy children! And in this love He rejoices over every insignificant saving act of ours. I ask you, what glory is it to the Lord and what benefit to you if you say a prayer that is distracted, or you do some small good deed such as making five prostrations, sighing, and calling on the name of Jesus Christ, or have a kind thought, or you deny yourself food or bear some difficulty in silence? All this will seem to you to be insignificant toward your salvation, and almost useless activity. But no! Every one of these small acts has value and will be counted by the all-seeing eye of God and will receive a hundredfold reward, not only in eternity but also in this life. St. John Chrysostom confirms this when he says, 'No act, however small, will be slighted by the just Judge.' If sins are counted with such detail that we have to give an account of all our words, desires, and thoughts, then how much more will our good deeds, no matter how small, be counted in great detail and turned into merit before our loving Judge.

"I will give you an example which I myself witnessed last year. There was a very devout and good monk in our Bessarabian monastery. One day a severe temptation came over him to get some smoked fish. There was no way he could get it in the monastery, so he planned to go to market where he could buy it. For a long time he experienced an inner struggle as he tried to tell himself that he should be satisfied with the common fare of the brothers, that as much as possible he should try to avoid self-indulgence, and that to go to market among throngs of people is not becoming to a monk and could be source of temptation to people. But in the end the temptation won out over his reason and he went to buy the fish.

"He left the monastery, and as he walked down the road, he realized that he did not have his rosary with him. How can I go like a soldier without his sword? he thought; this is unbecoming; the lay people that I will meet will be scandalized to see me without my rosary. He wanted to return to get the rosary, but he placed his hand in his pocket and found that he had it with him. He took it out, blessed himself, put it on his hand, and went on peacefully. As he came close to the market, he noticed a horse and wagon, filled with huge tubs, outside one of the shops. Suddenly something frightened the horse and he flung his hoofs into the air and then galloped away with the wagon, brushing against the monk as he did so and knocking him down, though not hurting him very much. A few steps beyond the monk the wagon overturned and was shattered into smithereens. The monk got up quickly and, though he was scared, he marveled at how God had saved his life, for he realized that if the wagon had overturned only a second sooner he also would have been smashed into bits like the wagon. But he stopped thinking about this and went to buy the fish.

"Then he returned home, ate the fish, said his prayers, and went to sleep. While asleep he had a vision of a stranger, an elder in his glory, who said to him, 'I am the patron of this monastery, brother, and I want you to understand and remember the lesson given to you today. You weakened in your struggle with the temptation for sensual pleasure and your laziness and lack of understanding of self-renunciation made it convenient for the enemy, who had planned the fatal accident which you witnessed, to come to you. But your guardian angel foresaw this, reminded you about the rosary, and inspired you to say a prayer, and as you responded to this inspiration positively and acted upon it, that very action saved you from death. Do you see how God loves man, and how generously He rewards even a small act of turning toward Him?' Having said this, the elder disappeared from the cell and the monk awoke just as he was bowing to the elder and he found himself not on his bed but on his knees at the threshold of the door. For their spiritual good, the monk told many people about this vision, including me.

"How infinite is God's love toward us sinners! Is it not surprising that for such a small act as taking out his rosary, calling on the name of God, and placing the rosary on his hand his life was spared? On the scales of justice one short minute of calling on the name of Jesus Christ outweighed many hours lost in slothfulness. Truly a mite here was rewarded with a gold piece. Do you see, brother, how powerful prayer is and how mighty is the name of Jesus Christ when we call on it? St. John Carphatos writes in the *Philokalia* that, when in reciting the Jesus Prayer we say, 'Have mercy on me a sinner,' God secretly answers every petition with, 'Child, your sins are forgiven.' And he says further that at the time when we pray we do not differ from the saints, the blessed, and the martyrs. And St. John Chrysostom says that the sinful man becomes pure at the moment when he says the Prayer. God's mercy toward us is boundless and we negligent sinners are not willing to give even a short hour to praising and thanking Him. The time of prayer, which is more important than anything else, we give to worldly cares and concerns, forgetting God and our debt to Him! For this reason we are often subject to troubles and misfortunes, but even these God in His loving providence intends for our spiritual good and our wholehearted return to Him."

When the merchant concluded his talk with the officer, I

said to him, "Dear brother, your talk brought great comfort to my sinful soul and I thank you for it."

He then began addressing himself to me. "It is obvious that you have an interest in spiritual matters," he said. "Wait a minute and I will read for you something very similar to what I have just said. I have with me a valuable book entitled *Agapia* or *The Salvation of Sinners*. It contains accounts of many extraordinary happenings."

So he took the book out of his pocket and began reading a beautiful story about a very devout man, Agaphonik, who was taught by his pious parents, while still a child, to pray daily one Hail Mary before the icon of the Mother of God. As a child he was very faithful to this practice, but when he grew up and was living on his own he became preoccupied with worldly cares and concerns and said the prayer less frequently and then in the end gave it up altogether. One evening there came to stay overnight at his house a stranger who identified himself as the hermit from Phabaid and who claimed that he had a vision in which he was told to come to Agaphonik and reproach him for neglecting his prayer to the Mother of God. Agaphonik presented his reasons for giving it up: for many years he was faithful to it and he did not see what good it did. The hermit said to him, "Blind and ungrateful man; you should remember how many times it protected you from trouble and misfortune. Do you remember how you were miraculously saved from drowning when you were a child? Do you remember how many of your neighbors went to the grave because of an epidemic and you were spared? Do you remember traveling with a friend and how both of you fell off the wagon and your friend broke his leg but you were unhurt? Do you know that an acquaintance of yours who was once young and healthy is withering away with sickness and you are without any suffering?" The hermit reminded Agaphonik of other things also and then concluded, "Know that all those misfortunes were turned away from you by the protection of the Mother of God for a short prayer with which you daily raised your soul to God. So keep on saying it and do not neglect it; continue to glorify the Heavenly Queen so that she can continue to protect you."

At the end of this reading our hosts called us to dinner, and after we received some nourishment, we thanked our benefactors and parted, each one going in his own direction.

I continued my journey for five days and found comfort in remembering the accounts I heard from the pious merchant of Byelaya Tserkov. But then, for some unknown reason, as I was approaching Kiev I experienced heaviness, weakness, and gloomy thoughts; slothfulness came upon me and it was difficult for me to pray. Not far from the road I saw a wooded area and I decided to find myself a quiet place to read the *Philokalia* and in that way strengthen my weak soul and regain my peace. I found a quiet place and began reading the Eight Thoughts by Cassian of Rome in the fourth part of the *Philokalia*. After joyously reading for about half an hour, I looked up and unexpectedly saw a man on his knees in the depths of the forest, some hundred yards away. I was glad to see this and thought that the man must certainly be praying and I continued with my reading. After an hour or more I again glanced in that direction and saw that he was still on his knees motionless. I was deeply touched by this and thought what devout servants of God there are. While I was thinking thus, the man fell to the ground and lay still. I was surprised to see this and, as I could not see his face since he knelt with his back to me, curiosity got the best of me and I went over to him to find out what kind of a man was praying in such a manner. As I came toward him I noticed that he was in light sleep. He was a country fellow about twenty-five years old, clean, good-looking, but pale. He was dressed in a peasant's caftan which was tied with a cord made of bast, and he had nothing with him, no knapsack and no staff. My steps awakened him and he got up. I asked him who he was, and he told me that he was a peasant from the Smolensky province on his way from Kiev.

"And where are you going?" I asked.

"I don't know myself, I guess wherever God leads me," he answered.

"Have you been away from home for a long time?"

"Yes, this is the fifth year."

"And where did you live during this time?"

"I visited holy places, monasteries, and churches. I have no one to live with as I am an orphan and with a crippled leg at that, so I wander from place to place."

"Apparently some wise person directed you to visit holy places and not simply to roam anywhere," I said.

"Well, you see, I have been an orphan since I was a little boy, and I was a shepherd in our village for ten years, during which time all went well. Then one day I brought home the herd of sheep without realizing that the best sheep of the headman was missing.

"Our headman was ill-tempered and mean, so when he came home that evening and saw that his sheep was missing, he came to me and abused me verbally and threatened what he would do to me if I didn't find his sheep. 'I will beat you to death; I'll break your arms and legs,' he said.

"So, frightened, I went looking for the lost sheep in all those places where the herd was grazing during the day. I searched and searched more than half the night, but there was no trace of it. The night was very dark, for it was almost autumn. When I came into the depths of the forest, which in our province is impassable, a storm blew up. It seemed to me that all the trees were swaying, and in the distance the wolves were howling. I became so frightened that my hair stood on end and every moment the terror seemed to increase and I thought I would die of dread. I threw myself on my knees, blessed myself, and with all my strength said, 'Lord Jesus Christ, have mercy on me.' As soon as I said these words, all fear left me and I was filled with peace. All my troubles disappeared as if they had never existed and I felt as wonderful as if I had flown to heaven. I was so happy that I continued to say the Prayer interiorly, and I don't remember how long the storm lasted or how I passed the night, for when I awoke it was already day and I was still on my knees. Then I got up peacefully and, knowing that I could not find the sheep, I went home feeling happy and having a great desire to continue to say the Prayer.

"When I came back to the village, the headman saw that I did not have his sheep and so he beat me half to death, and, as you see, he crippled my leg. After this beating I spent six weeks in bed, unable to move, but during all that time I was saying the Prayer and I was happy. When I regained my strength, I began to wander from place to place, but, as I found it very distracting and sinful in the world, I began visiting holy places and spending more time in the woods. It is now the fifth year that I have been doing this."

I was very happy to hear all this and I praised the Lord for making me worthy to meet such a holy man. Then I asked him, "Do you still recite the Prayer frequently?"

"Yes, it is impossible for me to be without it," he said. "When I remember how wonderful I felt that first time I said it in the forest, it seems that someone pushes me to my knees and I begin to pray again. But I do not know whether my sinful prayer is beneficial or not. Sometimes when I pray I feel great joy, peace, and comfort, not knowing what is the cause of this, and at other times I feel heaviness, boredom, and dejection. I am certain only of one thing—I want to continue to pray till I die."

"Do not be disturbed, beloved brother, because everything which you experience during the time of prayer is pleasing to God and beneficial toward your salvation. The holy Fathers say that both the comfort and the difficulty in prayer are good and that no prayer, regardless of how good or poor it is, is ever lost before God. Ease, warmth, and consolation indicate that God is rewarding our struggle in prayer, while heaviness, dejection, and dryness are meant to strengthen and purify the soul and by this means make it humble for the future taste of happiness and glory. In proof of this I will read to you from the writings of St. John Climacus."

I found the section and read it to him. He listened with attention and joy and thanked me profusely. And then we parted. He went into the depths of the forest, and I came on the road and continued with my journey, thanking God for making me, a sinner, worthy of such edification.

On the following day, with the help of God, I came to Kiev. My foremost desire was to fast and to prepare myself for confession and to receive the Holy Eucharist in this holy place, so I stayed close to the monastery, where it would be convenient for me to go to church. A good old Cossack took me into his home, and as he lived alone, I had peace and quiet. During the course of the week while preparing myself for confession, I resolved to make it a very detailed and thorough one and I began remembering the sins of my youth as well as all the others. In order not to forget anything, I wrote down everything that I could remember, to the smallest imperfection, and I ended up with a long list.

I heard that in the Kitayevaya Poustinia,[13] which is seven versts from Kiev, there was a priest of ascetical life who was very wise, prudent, and compassionate and that whoever went to him to confession received good advice and returned very happy. I was very glad to hear this and soon went to him. We talked for a while and then I gave him my list of sins to examine.

After reading the list, he said to me, "Beloved brother, you wrote here much that is useless. Listen, first, there is no need to confess again those sins which were previously confessed and for which you received absolution unless you have repeated them; otherwise it is a lack of faith in the power of the sacrament of penance. Second, there is no need to mention other people associated with your sins. You should only judge yourself. Third, the holy Fathers recommend that we confess our sins in general only, because relating things in detail could be a source of temptation both for oneself and for the confessor. Fourth, you came to repent, but you are not repenting of the fact that you do not know how to repent; your repentance is cold and careless. And, fifth, you enumerated all the trivialities but ignored the most important thing; you did not reveal your serious sins. You did not acknowledge and did not write down that you don't love God, that you hate your neighbor, that you do not believe in the word of

God, and that you are full of pride and ambition. The entire abyss of evil and of our spiritual corruption lies in these four sins. They are the main roots from which spring the shoots of all our other failings."

I was very surprised to hear this and said, "Forgive me, Reverend Father, but how is it possible not to love God, our Creator and Benefactor! What is there to believe in if not the word of God; it contains all truth and holiness. And I wish good to every man and have no reason to hate anyone. I have nothing to be proud of besides my innumerable sins and there is nothing in me worthy of praise. How could I be proud and ambitious in my poverty and sickness? Maybe if I were educated and rich I could be guilty of what you have suggested."

"It is unfortunate, beloved brother, that you understood so little of what I explained to you. To help you understand what I have said I will give you a list which I also use when I make my confession. Read it and you will see clearly all that I have just told you."

The priest gave me the guide to confession and I began reading it.

The Confession of an Interior Man, Leading to Humility

Turning my gaze at myself and attentively observing the course of my interior life I am convinced, through experience, that I love neither God nor my neighbor, that I have no faith, and that I am full of pride and sensuality. This realization is the result of careful examination of my feelings and actions.

1. *I do not love God.* For if I loved Him, then I would be constantly thinking of Him with heartfelt satisfaction; every thought of God would fill me with joy and delight. On the contrary, I think more and with greater eagerness about worldly things, while thoughts of God present difficulty and aridity. If I loved Him, then my

prayerful communion with Him would nourish, delight, and lead me to uninterrupted union with Him. But on the contrary, not only do I not find my delight in prayer but I find it difficult to pray; I struggle unwillingly, I am weakened by slothfulness and am most willing to do anything insignificant only to shorten or end my prayer. In useless occupations I pay no attention to time; but when I am thinking about God, when I place myself in His presence, every hour seems like a year. When a person loves another, he spends the entire day unceasingly thinking about his beloved, imagining being with him, and worrying about him; no matter what he is occupied with, the beloved does not leave his thoughts. And I in the course of the day barely take one hour to immerse myself deeply in meditation about God and enkindle within myself love for Him, but for twenty-three hours with eagerness I bring fervent sacrifices to the idols of my passions! I greatly enjoy conversations about vain subjects which degrade the spirit, but in conversations about God I am dry, bored, and lazy. And if unwillingly I am drawn into a conversation about spiritual matters, I quickly change the subject to something which flatters my passions. I have avid curiosity about secular news and political events; I seek satisfaction for my love of knowledge in worldly studies, in science, art, and methods of acquiring possessions. But the study of the law of the Lord, knowledge of God, and religion does not impress me, does not nourish my soul. I judge this to be an unessential activity of a Christian, a rather supplementary subject with which I should occupy myself in my leisure time. In short, if love of God can be recognized by the keeping of His commandments—"If anyone loves me he will keep my word," says the Lord Jesus Christ (John 14:23), and I not only do not keep His commandments but I make no attempt to do so—then in very truth I should conclude that I do not love God. St. Basil the Great confirms this when he says, "The evidence that man does not love God and His Christ is that he does not keep His commandments."

2. *I do not love my neighbor.* Not only because I am not ready to lay down my life for the good of my neighbor, according to the Gospel, but I will not even sacrifice my peace and my happiness for his good. If I loved my neighbor as myself, as the Gospel commands, then his misfortune would grieve me also and his prosperity would bring me great joy. But, on the contrary, I listen with curiosity to accounts of my neighbor's misfortune and I am not grieved but indifferent to them and, what is more, I seem to find satisfaction in them. I do not sympathize with the failings of my brother but I judge them and publicize them. My neighbor's welfare, honor, and happiness do not delight me as my own; I am either completely indifferent to them or I am jealous or envious.

3. *I do not have faith in spiritual realities.* I believe neither in immortality nor in the Gospel. If I were firmly convinced and believed without a doubt in eternal life and in retribution for our earthly actions, then I would be constantly thinking about this; the very thought of immortality would inspire me with wonder and awe and I would live my life as an alien who is getting ready to enter his native land. On the contrary, I don't even think of eternity and I consider the end of this life as the limit of my existence. I nurture a secret thought within and wonder, "Who knows what will happen after death?" Even when I say that I believe in immortality, it is only from natural reasoning, for down deep in my heart I am not convinced of it and my actions and preoccupations with earthly cares prove this. If I accepted the Holy Gospel with faith into my heart as the word of God, then I would be constantly occupied with it; I would study it, would delight in it, and with deep reverence would immerse myself in it. Wisdom, mercy, and love hidden within it would lead me to ecstasy, and day and night I would delight in the lessons contained in the law of God. They would be my daily spiritual bread and I would earnestly strive to fulfill them; nothing on

earth would be strong enough to keep me from this. But on the contrary, even if I sometimes read or listen to the word of God, it is either out of necessity or curiosity; I do not delve deeply into it but feel dryness and indifference to it and I receive no greater benefit from it than I do from secular reading. Further, I am eager to give it up promptly and go to worldly reading, in which I have greater interest and from which I get more satisfaction.

4. *I am full of pride and self-love*. All my actions confirm this. When I see something good in myself, then I wish to display it or brag about it to others, or interiorly I am full of self-love even when outwardly I feign humility. I ascribe everything to my own ability and I consider myself more perfect than others, or at least not worse. If I notice a vice in myself, then I try to excuse it or justify it; I pretend to be innocent or I claim that I couldn't help it. I am impatient with those who do not show me respect and I consider them incapable of judging character. I am vain about my talents and cannot accept any failure in my actions. I grumble and I am glad to see the misfortune of my enemies, and my intention in doing anything good is either praise, self-interest, or earthly comfort. In a word, I continuously make an idol out of myself, to whom I give unceasing service as I seek sensual delights and try to nourish my carnal desires.

Studying the guide to confession leads me to conclude that I am proud, adulterous, without faith; I do not love God and hate my neighbor. What state could be more sinful? The state of the spirits of darkness is better than my condition, for though they do not love God and hate man and are nourished by pride, at least they believe and tremble. But I? Can there be a worse fate than I am faced with? What is more strictly forbidden that man will be judged on than the careless and slothful life which I recognize in myself!

When I finished reading the guide to confession, I was astonished and thought to myself, My God, what terrible sins are hidden within me and up to this time I did not notice them! An ardent desire to be purified of them led me to ask this holy priest for direction so that I could get to the root cause of this evil and thus improve my life. And so the priest began to explain things to me.

"You see, beloved brother, the cause of the lack of love of God is lack of faith, and lack of faith is due to lack of conviction, which in turn is due to negligence in seeking clear and true knowledge and an indifference to spiritual enlightenment. In a word, not to believe is not to love, and not to be convinced is not to believe. But to be convinced, it is necessary to gain a detailed and thorough knowledge of a given subject; it is necessary to study and seriously reflect on the word of God and learn by experience to arouse in the soul a thirst and longing or, as some would say, 'an awe,' which then leads to an insatiable desire to know things more truly and penetrate their nature more deeply. One spiritual writer explains it in this way: 'Love,' he says, 'usually develops through knowledge, and the more depth and scope the knowledge has, the more love there will be and the easier it will be for the soul to open itself to God's love as it contemplates the most perfect and sublime Godhead and His infinite love for mankind.'

"Now you can see that the root cause of the sins you read about is slothfulness, which keeps a person from studying the spiritual realities and stifles the very desire for this. If you want to know how to overcome this evil, then by every possible means seek spiritual enlightenment. You can do this by diligent study of the word of God and the writings of the Fathers, by contemplation, by asking questions about Christ of the wise, and by spiritual direction. Ah, beloved brother, how many misfortunes we meet in life because we are too lazy to enlighten our soul with the word of truth and because we do not study the law of God day and night and pray about it diligently and persistently! Because of this our interior man is hungry, cold, and exhausted, having no strength to walk soberly on the path of truth toward salvation. Therefore, beloved brother, let us resolve to profit by these methods and as much as possible fill our minds with thoughts of heavenly things, and love, which is being poured into our hearts from above, will burst into flame. Let us do this together and let us pray as much as possible, for prayer is the chief and most powerful means of our renewal and transformation. We will pray as the church teaches: 'Lord, make me worthy to love you as much as I loved sin in the past!' "

I listened attentively to all this and then earnestly asked this saintly priest to hear my confession and give me the Holy Eucharist. In the morning, after being worthy to receive this blessed nourishment, I was ready to return to Kiev, but this good Father had plans to visit the Lavra Monastery for several days and he allowed me to stay in his cell, where, in solitude, I could give myself more fervently to prayer. And indeed, I spent those days as it were in heaven: Because of the prayers of my elder, I, unworthy sinner, enjoyed great peace. The Prayer flowed with such ease and sweetness in my heart that during this time I seemed to forget absolutely everything, even myself; my mind was totally immersed in Christ!

When the priest returned, I asked for his advice as to where I should continue my pilgrim's journey. He blessed me and said, "Go to the shrine at Pochaev to venerate the miraculous footprint of the immaculate Mother of God, and she will direct your steps on the path of peace." I received this guidance with faith and in three days headed for Pochaev.

For about two hundred versts I walked rather dejectedly as I saw no Christian dwellings along the road but only Jewish settlements and some taverns. Then I was glad to notice a Christian inn on one farm, and I stopped there to ask for lodging as well as for some bread for the road, for I had very little in my bag.

The owner of the inn was an old, but seemingly prosperous man who, like myself, came from the Orlovsky province. The moment I entered the room, he asked me, "Of what faith are you?"

I replied that I am an Orthodox Christian.

"Orthodox indeed," he sneered. "You have orthodoxy only on your lips, but in action you are apostates. I know your faith, brother! I was lured by one learned priest into your Church, but after six months I returned to our fellowship. It is most distracting to worship in your Church. The lectors skip parts of the Liturgy, and they mumble the rest so that they cannot be understood; the singers are no better than those in the village or in the tavern; and there is disorder in the way people stand, women together with men; they talk during the Liturgy, look around, and walk back and forth so that you cannot say your prayers in peace. What kind of a Liturgy is that? It is a sin! In our Church the Liturgy is celebrated with reverence; there is no skipping of parts, and the words are said distinctly; the music is touching; and the people stand in silence, men on one side and women on the other side; and all know when and what kind of a bow to make according to the regulations of the holy Church. Indeed, when you come into our Church you feel that you are attending a divine service, but in your Church it is not clear whether one is in the house of God or at a market!"

When I heard all this, I realized that the man was an Old Believer,[14] but because he spoke to the point I could not argue with him or try to convert him. I only thought to myself that at this time it is impossible to convert Old Believers to the true Church. First we must improve our church services, and the clerics especially should take a lead in this. The Old Believers are preoccupied with the external aspects of worship and they don't seem to be aware of the interior man, while we are careless about the externals.

And so I decided to leave this place, but just as I came into the hall I unexpectedly saw an open door into a private room, where a man who did not look Russian was lying on the bed and reading a book. He noticed me, called me in, and asked me who I was and I told him. He then said, "Listen, friend, wouldn't you work for me, a sick man, for about a week until with God's help I regain my health and strength? I am a Greek monk from Mount Athos who came to Russia to collect some funds for our monastery, and now on my return home I have become ill and I have such pain in my legs that I cannot walk; this is why I took a room here. Please do not refuse me, servant of God! I will pay you."

"There is no need for you to pay me," I replied. "I will gladly help you in whatever way I can for the sake of the Lord."

And so I stayed with him. I heard a great deal about spiritual matters from him; he talked about Mount Athos and about the holy ascetics, hermits, and recluses. He had a copy of the *Philokalia* in Greek as well as a book by Isaac of Syria, and we read together and compared the Slavonic translation of the *Philokalia* by Paissy Velichkovsky with the Greek original. He claimed that it is not possible to translate the *Philokalia* from the Greek more accurately than Velichkovsky did into the Slavonic.

I noticed that he prayed constantly and that he was experienced in the interior prayer of the heart, and as he spoke Russian well, I asked him about this subject. He eagerly shared his ideas with me, and I listened attentively and even wrote some things down. He explained the excellence and the greatness of the Jesus Prayer in the following way:

"The greatness of the Jesus Prayer is revealed in its very form, which consists of two parts. The first part, 'Lord Jesus Christ, Son of God,' leads the mind into the history of the life of Jesus Christ, or as the Fathers explain, it contains within itself the short form of the Gospel. And the second part, 'have mercy on me a sinner,' tells the story of our weakness and sinfulness in an extraordinary way because it is not possible for a poor, humble, and sinful soul to express its petition more fundamentally and precisely. Every other petition would not be as comprehensive and all-inclusive. For example, if one were to say, 'Forgive me, cleanse me from my sins, free me from my transgressions, blot out my offenses,' all of these words would express only one petition, prompted by fear and coming from a cowardly and negligent soul who wishes to be freed from punishment. But the expression 'have mercy on me' not only sets forth the petition for forgiveness, which is the result of fear, but is a sincere cry of filial love and trust in the mercy of God; it is a cry of a soul humbly aware of its weakness and lack of control in its vigilance over self. It is a cry for pardon, grace, and strength from God to overcome temptation and to conquer one's sinful inclinations. This can be compared to a poor debtor asking his gracious creditor not only to excuse his debt but, considering his poverty, to give him alms. This profound expression, 'have mercy on me,' says as it were, 'Gracious Lord! Forgive me my sins and help me to improve my life; give me an ardent desire to do your will and convert my mind, my heart and will to you alone.'"

I was deeply impressed by his wisdom, and I thanked him for edifying my sinful soul.

Then he explained another remarkable thing to me. "If you wish," he said, "then I will tell you about the different inflections of the Jesus Prayer." And he did so in a scholarly way, for he studied at the Academy of Athens. "I have had the opportunity to hear many God-fearing Christians recite the Jesus Prayer vocally both at home and in church, according to the precept of the Lord and the teaching of the Church. If one listens attentively to this whispered form of the Prayer, it is possible to note and to be inspired by the fact that the tone of the Prayer differs from person to person. For example, some people raise their voice on the very first word of the Prayer, Lord, and all the rest of the words they finish on an even lower tone. Others begin the Prayer on a lower tone, raise their voice in the middle of the Prayer on the word Jesus, which they say a bit louder, and then finish the rest on a lower tone as they had begun. Still others say most of the Prayer on a lower tone and raise their voice only on the phrase Son of God. And finally some say the Prayer on a lower tone until the phrase Have mercy on me, which they exclaim in ecstasy.

"Now look, the Prayer is one and the same; Orthodox Christians have the same general belief that this most important and sublime Prayer consists of two realities—the Lord Jesus and man's appeal to His mercy, which is known to all. Why then do they not all intone it the same way? Why not stress one and the same word or phrase? Why the individual

difference in stress? Some will say that this is the result of
habit or that people copy one another or that it shows how
each individual understands the Prayer or finally that the
difference depends on the individual's facility with words.
But my idea on this is completely different. I see in this
difference something greater, something which is hidden not
only from those who listen but even from those who pray.
Isn't this the secret movement of the Holy Spirit, who makes
intercession for us with unspeakable groanings when we know
not how and for what to pray? And if everyone prays in the
name of Jesus Christ by the Holy Spirit, as the Apostle Paul
writes, then the Spirit who works in secret gives prayer to the
one who prays and gives his gifts to all despite their lack of
strength. To one he gives reverential fear, to another the gift
of love, to still another firmness of faith, real humility, etc.
And therefore, he who has received the gift to revere and
glorify the power of the Almighty expresses the word *Lord*
with special feeling and delight, for in this word he recognizes the grandeur and the power of the Creator of the
world. He who has received a secret outpouring of love into
his heart is filled with sweetness and delight as he exclaims
Jesus Christ; this is what a certain elder experienced who was
filled with great love and delight whenever he heard the
name of Jesus even in ordinary conversation. In him who has
steadfast faith in the divinity of Jesus Christ, who is one with
God the Father, the Spirit enkindles even greater faith when
he expresses the words *Son of God*. And finally he who has
the gift of humility and deep awareness of his weakness utters
the words *have mercy on me* with great intensity; humble
and contrite, he abhors his failings and nourishes his hope
with God's mercy. In my opinion these are the reasons for
the various inflections in the recitation of the Prayer in the
name of our Lord Jesus Christ! Therefore it is possible while
one listens to the Prayer to understand and to be aware, for
the glory of God and one's own edification, what sentiment
and what gift is being expressed. In regard to this subject
some people have asked me, 'Why are the hidden gifts of the
Holy Spirit not manifested as one, so that every word of the

Prayer would be permeated with delightful sweetness?' And my reply was that God distributes His gifts wisely and according to each one's strength, as the Holy Scripture testifies; so who can fathom the mystery of grace with the finite mind? Is not the clay in the full power of the potter, and is he not free to do what he chooses with it?"

I spent five days with this elder, and his health gradually improved. This time was so spiritually profitable for me that I wasn't even aware of how quickly it passed. The little room was like a hermitage where the two of us either prayed, calling on the name of Jesus, or talked about prayer and interior life.

One day a pilgrim stopped by who complained bitterly about the Jews. He claimed that when he passed through their settlements he was mistreated and deceived. He felt so embittered against them that he cursed them and even regarded them unworthy to live on earth because of their stubbornness and unbelief. He acknowledged that he had an insurmountable aversion toward them. Hearing this, my new friend, the elder, endeavored to bring this man to a better understanding.

"My friend," he said, "there is no sense in your abusing and cursing the Jews. They are also creatures of God like we are, and you should be in sympathy with them and pray for them and not abuse them. Believe that your hatred is caused by the fact that you are not firmly grounded in the love of God and you are not interiorly secure and at peace with yourself. I will read something for you from the holy Fathers. Listen to what Mark the Ascetic says: 'The soul which is interiorly united with God is full of joy and like a gentle and simplehearted child does not judge anyone, neither the Greek, the pagan, the Jew, nor the sinner, but looks at everyone without exception with a pure eye, rejoices with the whole world, and desires that all, Greeks, Jews and pagans, praise God.' And Macarius the Great of Egypt says that real contemplatives are burning with such great love that, if it were possible, they would take every man into their bosom, not separating the good from the evil. Do you hear, beloved brother, how the holy Fathers judge? I would therefore advise you to get rid of your hostility and learn to look at everything as it really is in the plan of the all-knowing God, and when you meet with affronts, see in them opportunities for learning patience and humility."

Now more than a week had passed and the elder was well again. I thanked him heartily for all the edifying instructions and then we parted. He went home and I went on my proposed journey.

I was getting close to Pochaev, but before I covered a hundred versts some sort of a soldier caught up with me. I asked him where he was going, and he replied that he was on his way to visit relatives in the Kamenets Podolsky province.

For about ten versts we walked in silence and I noticed his heavy breathing and his dejection, so I asked him, "What is the cause of your grief?"

He came closer to me and said, "Good man! since you have noticed my grief, I will tell you all about it if you will swear not to disclose it to anyone; my death is approaching and I need to speak with someone."

I assured him, in a Christian manner, that there was no reason for me to carry anything to anyone and that in brotherly love I would give him whatever advice I could.

"You see," he said, "I was drafted from the state peasants into the army. While in the service I was often thrashed for drunkenness and misconduct, and after five years I found the life there so unbearably difficult that I decided to defect. It has now been fifteen years that I have been a fugitive. For six years I hid here and there; I stole from storerooms and warehouses; on my own I stole horses and broke into stores. The stolen goods I sold to various swindlers, and the money I spent on drink. I led a depraved life and committed every kind of sin except that I did not ruin any souls. For a while things went well, and then I was thrown into jail for wandering without a passport. But when I had the chance, I ran away from there also.

"Then one day, unexpectedly, I met a soldier with a clean record who was on his way home from the army to a faraway province. He was sick and could hardly walk, so he asked me to help him, to bring him to the nearest village where he could find a place to stay. I did this. We made it to a village, where the police gave us permission to sleep in a barn on some hay, and that is where we lay down. In the morning when I woke up, I saw that my soldier friend was dead and stiff. Quickly I searched for his passport and his discharge papers, with which I also found quite a bit of money, and while everyone was still asleep, I quickly left the barn and through the back yard escaped into the forest. When I examined the soldier's passport, I noted that his age and distinguishing characteristics were similar to mine. This made me happy and I went courageously into the depths of the Astrakhan province. There I got myself a job as a laborer and settled down. I lodged with an old man who was a cattle dealer and had his own house. This man lived alone with his widowed daughter, and after I stayed with them for a year, I married the daughter. But soon the old man died. My wife and I could not manage the business, and I began drinking again. My wife also started drinking, and within a year we spent everything that was left by the old man. Finally my wife also became ill and died, so I sold everything, including the house, and in short time I squandered all that money. Now I had nothing to live on, nothing to buy my bread with, and so I resumed my former way of life and began dealing in stolen goods and with greater courage than before because I now had a passport. I did this for about a year, but I was not always successful.

"One time I stole an old horse from a poor peasant and sold it to a flaying house for fifty kopecks. With that money I went to a tavern to get some wine, and while drinking I decided on a plan: I would go to a certain village where there was a wedding celebration going on, and after the banquet, when all the people went to sleep, I would steal whatever I could get my hands on. But as the sun had not yet set, I went into the woods to wait for the night. I lay down and fell into deep sleep. I had a dream in which I saw myself standing in a beautiful and spacious meadow, when suddenly

I noticed an ominous cloud in the sky and, shortly after, such a loud clap of thunder followed that the earth opened up under me and someone seemed to hammer me into the ground up to my shoulders. I was wedged in from all sides, and only my head and hands were outside. Then the foreboding cloud came down to the ground, and my grandfather, who had been dead for twenty years, stepped out of it. He was a devout man and was a churchwarden for some thirty years. I shook with fear as he came close to me, for he had an angry and threatening expression on his face. On the ground around me I saw heaps of objects which I had stolen at various times. This terrified me even more.

"My grandfather came close to me, pointed to the first heap and said, 'What is that? Let him have it.'

"And I felt such a terrific pressure of the ground on all sides of me that in unbearable pain I moaned and cried, 'Have mercy!'

"But the torments continued and my grandfather pointed to another heap and said, 'And what is that? Torture him even more!'

"And I experienced still more torments so that no suffering of this world could be compared to it.

"Finally, my grandfather brought the old horse close to me, the one which I had stolen only yesterday, and he shouted, 'And what is that? Torture him to the utmost!'

"And I was so crushed from every side that I cannot even begin to describe the cruel torments and agony which I experienced. It seemed that my sinews were being pulled out of my body and the pain was so unbearable that had it continued a bit longer I would have lost consciousness; but then the horse kicked me in the cheek and at that moment I woke up, terrified and shaking like a leaf. I noticed that the sun was rising, that it was daylight; I touched my cheek and it was bleeding and all those parts of my body which in the dream were in the ground were stiff and painful. Terribly frightened, I got up somehow and went home. The cheek hurt me for a long time and you can see that I have a scar, which before this incident I did not have.

"After this vision fear and terror often overwhelmed me; I would just recall the torments of that dream and such agony and depression took hold of me that I did not know what to do with myself. With time the thought of this vision tormented me even more and I began to fear people and to feel as ashamed as if everyone knew about my knavery. Because of this melancholy state I could not eat, drink, or sleep and I reeled like a shadow. I thought of going to my regiment and confessing everything; perhaps if I accept punishment, God would forgive me my sins, but I was afraid that I might have to run the gauntlet so I gave up that idea. I came to the end of my patience and I wanted to hang myself, but I thought that I do not have long to live anyway since I lost all my strength, so I decided to go home and say good-bye to my relatives and then die there. I have a nephew in my hometown and I am on my way there. I have been on the road for six months now with dejection and fear as my companions. So what do you think, good man? What should I do? I have had more than my share of suffering."

Hearing all this, I wondered within myself and praised the wisdom of God which directs sinners by such diverse paths, and I said to him, "Beloved brother, in your fear and dejection you should pray to God; prayer is the main form of healing of all our troubles."

"But I cannot pray," he said to me. "I think that the moment that I begin to pray God will destroy me."

"Nonsense, brother! Such thoughts are from the evil one. God is infinitely merciful and sympathizes with the sinner; He is eager to forgive anyone who repents. If you know the Jesus Prayer, that is 'Lord Jesus Christ, have mercy on me a sinner,' then say it without ceasing."

"Yes, I certainly know that Prayer! When I went to steal, I sometimes said it to get courage."

"You see, God did not destroy you then when you were going to do wrong and said the Prayer, so how could He harm you now when you say it on the road to repentance? Now you can see that your thoughts are from the enemy! Believe, beloved brother, that if you will say this Prayer, disregarding all thoughts that come to your mind, you will soon experience comfort; all fear and heaviness will pass and in the end you will have great peace. You will become a devout man and all your sinful passions will disappear. I assure you of this because I have seen a great deal of it in my encounters with people."

With this I related some incidents to him in which the miraculous power of the Jesus Prayer was seen to transform sinners. Then I encouraged him to stop with me at the shrine of the Mother of God, the refuge of sinners, and there make his confession and receive the Holy Eucharist before going to his relatives. My soldier friend listened carefully and, as far as I could see, joyfully to all I said and agreed to my suggestion.

So we went together to Pochaev with an understanding that we would not talk but would ceaselessly recite the Jesus Prayer. We walked in silence for one day. On the following day he told me that he felt better, and it was quite obvious that he was more at peace. On the third day we came to Pochaev, and I continued to encourage him to recite the Prayer both day and night until he fell asleep. Further, I assured him that the holy name of Jesus is unbearable to the enemy and that it would certainly help him. Then I read for him from the *Philokalia* about the fact that it is particularly important to say the Jesus Prayer with great attention when we are preparing to receive the Holy Eucharist.

He continued to say the Prayer and soon went to confession and Communion. From time to time disturbing thoughts still assailed him, but with the Jesus Prayer he was now able to dispel them. In order to rise early for Sunday matins, he went to bed early but continued to recite the Jesus Prayer, and I sat in the corner and read the *Philokalia* by the night lamp. An hour passed and he fell asleep; and I began to pray.

After about twenty minutes he suddenly woke up, jumped up, and came to me with tears in his eyes, and with great joy he exclaimed, "Ah, brother, what I just saw! How very happy and at peace I am! Now I believe that God loves sinners and does not torment them. Glory be to You, Lord, glory be to You!"

I was surprised and happy to hear this and asked him to tell me in detail what happened to him.

"Here is what happened," he said. "As soon as I fell asleep, I saw myself in that same meadow where I was once tormented. At first I was scared, but then instead of the cloud I saw the sun rising; a strange light illumined the whole meadow and I saw beautiful flowers and grass. Then suddenly my grandfather came close to me and he looked so wonderful that you could not look at him long enough. Gently and lovingly he said to me, 'Go to Zhitomir to the Church of George the Triumphant. There you can work as a churchwarden. Live there till the end of your life and pray without ceasing. God will have mercy on you and will bless you!' After saying this he made the sign of the cross on me and disappeared. I cannot even describe the great joy that I felt; it was as if a great burden had been removed from my shoulders and I flew to heaven. I woke up feeling ecstatic; I was beside myself with joy. Now I know what to do. I will go immediately to Zhitomir, where my grandfather directed me to go. With the Prayer it will be easy for me to walk."

"For goodness' sake, beloved brother, where will you go in the middle of the night? Stay for matins, and then you can go on your way with God."

So we did not sleep but after this conversation we went to church. During the entire matins he prayed with great devotion and tears and said how delightful and easy it was to say the Jesus Prayer. Then during the Liturgy he received the Holy Eucharist again, and after lunch I went with him as far as the road to Zhitomir, where with joyful tears we parted.

Now I wondered about my direction: Where should I go? I decided that I would go back to Kiev. It would be good to visit that wise priest there and perhaps after I stayed with him for a while he would find me a benefactor who would help me to get to Jerusalem or at least to Mount Athos. I stayed in Pochaev another week, thinking about the instructive encounters I had had on my journey and writing down some of the edifying examples. Then I got ready for the road. I put on my knapsack and went to church to attend the Liturgy before leaving and to ask the Mother of God to bless my journey.

While I stood in the back of the church, some man came in who seemed to be of noble birth though he was not too well dressed. He asked me where the candles were being sold and I showed him. After the Liturgy I stayed to pray at the shrine of the Mother of God, and when I finished my prayers I went on my way. As I walked down the street, I noticed a house with an open window by which a man was sitting and reading a book. I had to pass that way and as I came closer I recognized the man; he was the one who had asked me about the candles in church. I tipped my hat to him, and he beckoned to me and said, "No doubt you are a pilgrim." Then he invited me in and asked me who I was and where I was going. He offered me some tea and said, "Listen, brother, I would suggest that you go to the Solovecky Monastery and specifically to the Anzersky Skete.[15] It is such an exceptionally quiet and peaceful spot that it is like a second Mount Athos. Everyone is welcome there who is willing to read the Psalter in church for four hours out of every twenty-four. I myself am going there and have made a vow to go on foot. We could go together, and it would be safer for me because people say that the road is very isolated. I have money and I would feed you for the whole trip; we could walk some distance apart so that we would not disturb one another's prayer. Think about it, brother, and I hope that you will agree, for it will be beneficial for you also."

I regarded this invitation as an answer to my prayer for direction to the Mother of God and I readily agreed to go with this man.

And so on the next day we began our walking journey. We walked for three days as we had agreed, some distance apart. He continuously read his book and never seemed to take it out of his hands both day and night, and at times he meditated on something. Then we stopped for lunch at one place. He ate, but the book remained opened before him and he frequently looked into it.

I saw then that it was the Gospel that he was reading, and I said to him, "May I be bold enough to ask you, brother, why you so constantly, both day and night, hold on to the Gospel? You never let it out of your hands."

"Because I am continuously learning something from the book," he answered.

"What are you learning?" I continued.

"That prayer is the essence of Christian life. I consider prayer the most important and necessary means of salvation and the first responsibility of every Christian. Because prayer is both the first step and the crown of a devout life, the Gospel directs man to pray constantly. A particular time is set for other deeds of devotion, but for prayer there is no appointed time; we should pray always. Without prayer it is impossible to do anything good, and without the Gospel it is impossible to learn the right form of prayer. Therefore, all those who received salvation through interior life, the preachers of the word of God, the hermits, and the recluses, and all God-fearing Christians ceaselessly studied the word of God; the reading of the Gospel was their essential activity. Many of them had a copy of the Gospel in their hands continuously, and if anyone asked them for guidance regarding salvation, they gave this advice. 'Sit in silence in your cell and read and reread the Gospel.'"

I was very pleased to hear his wise comments on prayer and to see his interest in it, so I asked him further, "From which Gospel in particular can one learn about prayer?"

"From all four Evangelists," he replied. "In a word, from reading the entire New Testament in order. After careful reading and rereading of the New Testament I discovered that the sacred writers present the teaching on prayer in a systematic way; that there is a gradual development and organic unity which begins in the writings of the first Evangelist and continues throughout the New Testament. For example, at the very beginning we have the introduction to prayer, then the form or the outward expression in words, then the

necessary conditions for prayer, then the method of learning
it and examples. Finally, the secret teaching about the interior and ceaseless prayer in the name of Jesus Christ is given
and it is shown to be higher than formal prayer; then man's
need of prayer, the fruits of prayer, etc. In a word everything,
complete and detailed knowledge about the exercise of
prayer, is given in a systematic way from the beginning to
end."

After hearing this, I decided to ask him to show me
specifically what he meant, and I said to him, "Nothing
pleases me more than to listen to talks about prayer, so I
would appreciate it if you would explain to me in detail the
mysterious unity in the teaching about prayer found in the
Gospel. For the sake of the Lord, please show it to me."

He readily agreed to this and said to me, "Open your New
Testament, look at it, and note what I will say." He gave me
a pencil, excused himself while he looked at his notes, and
then continued, "Now find chapter 6 of St. Matthew and
read verses 5 through 9. Here you can see the introductory
lesson on prayer. We are to pray with a pure intention and
not to impress others; we are to find a quiet place for our
prayer and ask for the forgiveness of our sins and union with
God; we are not to imitate the pagans and make up many petitions about the various needs of life. When you read verses
10 through 13 of this same chapter, you can see what the
form of our prayer should be, what type of words we should
use to express it. All the needs of our life are very wisely expressed in this prayer. Then in verses 14 and 15 of this same
chapter we can see what condition must be met to make our
prayer effective, for if we do not forgive those who have
offended us, then the Lord will not forgive us our sins. Verses
7 through 12 of chapter 7 show how we can succeed in
prayer and why we should be full of hope when we 'ask, seek,
and knock.' This forceful expression shows that prayer is to
have a pre-eminent place in our lives and that it is to be frequent; prayer is not only to accompany all our actions but is
to precede them in time. This is an important attribute of
prayer. You can see an example of this in chapter 14 of St.

Mark, verses 32 through 40, where Christ Jesus repeats the same prayer several times. Another example about frequent prayer can be seen in the Gospel of St. Luke chapter 11, verses 5 through 14, in the parable of the persistent friend and the importunate widow asking the judge for mercy. In chapter 18 of Luke's Gospel, verses 1 through 15, we have a command of Jesus Christ to pray always and in all places; we are not to lose heart or give in to slothfulness.

"In addition to this detailed instruction on prayer the Gospel of John contains the basic teaching regarding the interior prayer of the heart. This is introduced in the conversation of Jesus with the Samaritan woman, where Christ says that God is to be worshiped in spirit and in truth and where ceaseless prayer is presented as living water springing to life eternal (John 4:5–25). In verses 4 through 8 of chapter 15 there is a clearer illustration of the necessity and the power of interior prayer; the soul is to abide in Christ and is to be constantly aware of God's presence. And finally in chapter 16 of John, verses 23 through 25, there is a mystery revealed! You can see that prayer uttered in the name of Jesus Christ, or what we call the Jesus Prayer, 'Lord Jesus Christ, have mercy on me,' has great power and when it is repeated frequently it can easily sanctify and transform the heart. This can certainly be seen in the examples of the Apostles; they were Christ's disciples less than a year when He taught them the Our Father, which prayer they passed on to us, but at the end of His earthly life Jesus Christ revealed a mystery to them which they needed to know to be decisively successful in their prayer. He said to them, 'Until now you have not asked for anything in my name. Ask and you will receive, and so your joy will be complete' (John 16:24). And this is indeed what happened to them, for when the Apostles learned to pray in the name of the Lord Jesus Christ, they performed many miracles and were themselves transformed.

"Now do you see the logic, the fullness, and the wisdom with which the Gospel presents the teaching on prayer? And to learn still more about prayer we can read the letters of the Apostles.

"In continuing with our theme, I will point out some excerpts which illustrate the various aspects of prayer. Thus, in the Acts of the Apostles we read how the first Christians prayed, how their vibrant faith in Jesus Christ prompted them to pray continuously and fervently; and then we read that the result of this continuous abiding in prayer was the outpouring of the gifts of the Holy Spirit on those who prayed. A similar example is given in chapter 16, verses 25 and 26. Then looking at the letters of the Apostles we can see: first, that it is necessary to pray under all circumstances of life (Jas. 5:13–16); second, that the Holy Spirit helps us in our prayer (Jude 1:20 and Rom. 8:26); third, that it is necessary to pray in the Spirit on every occasion (Eph. 6:18); fourth, that calm and inner peace are necessary for prayer (Phil. 4:6–7); fifth, that it is necessary to pray without ceasing (1 Thess. 5:17); and, finally, that it is necessary to pray for everyone and not only for ourselves (1 Tim. 2:1–5).

"By careful and attentive reading of Scripture it is possible to find many more insights about prayer which are hidden from the casual or the superficial reader. From what I have shown you, have you noticed the gradual and systematic development in the instruction on prayer which we have from our Lord Jesus Christ in the New Testament? Do you see in what marvelous way it is distributed in all four Evangelists? In St. Matthew we see the introduction to prayer, the form, and the conditions; in St. Mark we find examples; in St. Luke, parables; and in St. John, the mysterious exercise of interior prayer; though either briefly or comprehensively this is presented in all four evangelists. The Acts present the practice and the results of prayer and the Letters and the Revelation the many aspects of the act of prayer. This then is the reason why I use only the New Testament to study the various ways leading to salvation."

All the references which he mentioned and explained I noted in my own Bible; everything seemed remarkable and inspiring to me and I thanked him wholeheartedly.

We continued to walk in silence for five more days. Then

my companion began to have trouble with his feet, perhaps because he was not accustomed to walking that much. And so he hired a wagon with two horses and took me with him. Today we arrived in your district and we will be here for three days to rest; then we will head for the Anzersky Skete, where my friend is eager to go.

"Your friend sounds remarkable," said the elder. "He must be both a very devout and a learned man and I would like to meet him."

"We are staying together, and so I will bring him to you tomorrow. Now it is too late. Good-bye."

CHAPTER 6

"Brother helped by brother is a fortress, friends are like the bars of a keep." (Prov. 18:19)

PILGRIM. As I promised yesterday, I have returned with my highly esteemed companion, the man who gladdened my pilgrim's journey by his inspiring conversation and whom you wished to meet.

ELDER. I am delighted to see both of you and, I hope, so are my honored guests; we are eager to hear of your experiences. Here are my guests: the honorable monk and the devout priest. We have Christ's word that where there are two or more gathered in His name, there He is among them, and since there are five of us assembled in His name, we can count on a most generous outpouring of His grace.

Beloved brother, the account your companion gave me yesterday of your ardent love of the holy Gospel is very remarkable and instructive; we are eager to learn by what method this holy mystery was revealed to you.

PROFESSOR. The all-loving God, who wishes all to come to the truth and to be saved, in His great mercy, revealed this knowledge to me in a most extraordinary way without any human intervention. For five years I was a professor at the lyceum and I led a rather dissipated life; my great interest was in secular and worldly philosophy rather than Christian. I could have perished spiritually if I had not been restrained to some degree by my devout mother and my serious-minded sister, with whom I lived.

One day when I was walking on the boulevard, I met and became acquainted with a very handsome young man; he told me that he was a French student and had only recently come from Paris and was seeking a job as a tutor. I was very impressed with the education of this stranger and I invited him to my house and we became friends. During the course of two months he visited me frequently and we went for walks, amused ourselves, and sometimes went to the most immoral places in search of company.

Once when he came with an invitation to visit such a place, he seemed particularly eager to convince me to go and was most extravagant in his praise of the happy atmosphere of the place he was inviting me to. But suddenly he stopped and asked me to leave my room and to join him in the living room. This seemed strange to me, and I said to him that more than once already I had noticed his reluctance to stay in my study and I asked him the reason for this. I detained him in my study and explained that the living room was close to my mother's and sister's room and that it would be most inappropriate for us to discuss our affairs there.

But he was firm in his desire to leave my room and finally said to me, "Well, on the shelf among your books you have a copy of the Gospel, and because I respect that book, it is difficult for me to speak about our unholy interests in its presence. Please take it out of here and then we will be free to speak."

In my foolishness I smiled at his words, took the Gospel from the shelf, and said to him, "You should have told me this a long time ago!" And giving him the Gospel, I said, "Here, you yourself can place it in that room."

The moment I touched him with the Gospel, he shuddered and then vanished. This so shocked me that I fell to the floor unconscious. My mother and sister heard the noise and came running, but for half an hour they could not bring me to consciousness. When I finally came to, trembling and all distraught, I seemed to be paralyzed, for I could not move my hands and feet. A doctor was called, who diagnosed my illness as paralysis caused by shock or fear.

For a whole year after this incident I lay in bed and was under the doctor's care, but there was not even the slightest

improvement in my sickness and I found it necessary to resign from my teaching profession. At this time my elderly
mother died and my sister decided to enter a religious community; and this fact made my illness even worse. I had only
one comfort during this time of my illness and that was reading the Gospel; from the beginning of my sickness it never
left my hands but served as a reminder of that mysterious
happening.

One day, very unexpectedly, a monk who was collecting
money for his monastery stopped by our house. He asked
about my illness and then told me very forcefully that I
should not put all my trust in medicine, which without the
help of God has no power to heal; he encouraged me to ask
God for help, to earnestly pray about my condition because
*prayer is the most powerful means of healing of all sickness,
both physical and spiritual.*

In my confusion, I objected, "How can I possibly pray in
this condition when I have no strength to make prostrations
or even to raise my hand for the sign of the cross?"

His only response was, "Make an effort to pray!" and he
gave me no further explanation of how I should pray.

After my guest left, almost against my will, I found myself
thinking about prayer, about its effects and its power. I began
to remember the theological lectures which I had heard a
long time ago when I was a student, and I found comfort in
recalling religious truths; they brought me comfort and I
began to feel some relief in my sickness. As the Gospel was
always with me, and I had faith in it because of the miraculous incident, I recalled that all the discourses on prayer
which I had heard at the lectures were based on the Gospel
texts, and so I began to study the precepts of the Gospel as
the best source of prayer and Christian devotion. By careful
reading, I discovered that the Gospel, as an abundant foun-
tain, contains all that is necessary for true interior prayer and
a holy life. Reverently I noted all the passages about this subject, and ever since that time I have been trying to learn and
understand as much as possible about these divine decrees. I
have also tried, though not without difficulty, to apply them

in my daily life. With such wholesome occupation my illness began to improve, and in the end, as you can see, I became completely well. Since I was living all alone, I decided that in gratitude to God for His fatherly mercy, for the healing of both my body and my mind, I would follow the inclination of my soul and the example of my sister and dedicate myself to a hermit's life. Such a life style would enable me to live the precepts of Scripture with greater ease.

So now I am on my way to the solitary Anzersky Skete of the Solovecky Monastery on the White Sea, which I have heard is a place most conducive to contemplative life. However, I would like to add in all honesty that, though the Gospel comforts me on my journey, enlightens my dull mind, and warms my cold heart, I have to acknowledge my doubts openly and admit that the conditions for holiness and salvation which demand such complete selflessness, extraordinary deeds, and deep humility frighten me by their very magnitude because of my weakness and my past sins. I stand between despair and hope and know not what awaits me in the future!

MONK. With so special a pledge and extraordinary mercy which you have received from God, and with your learning, it is unpardonable not only to fall into dejection but even to allow a shadow of a doubt into your soul about God's protection and His help. Do you know what St. John Chrysostom says about this? "No one should lose heart under the pretext that the precepts of the Gospel are too difficult or impossible of fulfillment. God wishes man to be saved, and the purpose of His commandments is not to make him an offender by reason of their difficulty. No! God's purpose is to reward us both here and hereafter for the keeping of His holy laws."

Of course, for our human nature consistent and unflinching effort in keeping God's laws seems extraordinarily difficult, and consequently salvation seems beyond man's reach; but sacred Scripture, which gives us God's law, also gives us the means to fulfill it easily and joyfully. If at a first glance this is veiled in mystery, it is, of course, to help us learn humility and come more readily to union with God by

spontaneously seeking refuge in prayer and asking God for
His fatherly help. Here then is the secret of man's salvation
and not in his reliance on his own efforts.

PILGRIM. Weak and feeble as I am, how I would like to
know that secret, so that at least to some degree I could direct my slothful life to the glory of God and the salvation of
my soul.

MONK. Beloved brother, you do know this secret from
your book, the *Philokalia*. It consists in ceaseless prayer,
which you have learned so well and which you fervently practice and find comfort in.

PILGRIM. Reverend Father, I beg you for a favor. For the
sake of the Lord, please make me worthy to hear from your
lips some insights about this saving mystery, this interior
prayer; I like nothing more than to read about prayer, and listen to discussions about it for the strengthening and comfort
of my sinful soul.

MONK. Because of my limited experience, I cannot satisfy
your desire and explain this sublime activity to you by my
own reasoning, but I do have an excellent article written by a
spiritual writer on this very subject. And if all here present
would like to hear it, then I will get it immediately and read
it for you.

ALL. Please do, Reverend Father. Do not keep such salutary knowledge from us.

THE MYSTERY OF SALVATION REVEALED THROUGH CEASELESS PRAYER

How does one attain salvation? This pious question comes
naturally to the mind of every Christian as a result of two
things: man's innate longing for truth and righteousness
and his awareness of his tainted and weakened human nature. Everyone, even the man with little faith in immortality and the rewards of afterlife, finds himself thinking about
salvation when he turns his glance toward heaven. But
being unable to come up with any answers, he questions

the wise and the experienced; he follows their advice and reads inspiring books of spiritual writers, and he tries resolutely to apply the truths and directives which he has learned. In one way or another all of these instructions show him the necessary conditions for salvation: a devout life, heroic actions, and complete self-renunciation. The practice of virtue and a wholehearted fulfillment of God's commandments are to bear witness to his firm and vibrant faith. Further, he learns that all of these conditions of salvation are to be fulfilled with deep humility and concurrently, because virtuous acts depend on one another, support one another, perfect and inspire one another. This process is similar to the rays of the sun, which only show their power and light when they are concentrated through a glass into one point. Scripture confirms this when it says that he who is unfaithful in little things is also unfaithful in bigger ones.

In addition to this, to convince him even more completely of the need to practice moral integrity, he hears of the tragedy of sin and of the excellence of virtue. All of this is strongly impressed on his mind with a promise of either a great reward of heavenly bliss or unspeakable punishment in eternity. This is the special character of modern preaching.

After hearing such instruction, the man who earnestly seeks salvation approaches the fulfillment of these directives with great joy and tries to apply and to experience all that he has read and heard. But alas! even in the first step of his attempt he seems incapable of reaching his goal. He sees and experiences his weakened nature taking the upper hand over the convictions of his mind, and he finds that his free will is constrained, his inclinations are sinful, and the power of his spirit is exhausted. In this awareness of his weakness he naturally wonders whether there is a method which would facilitate his striving for the perfection which the law of God enjoins on him, which Christian devotion demands, and which was fulfilled by those who were found worthy to attain salvation and holiness. And so, to reconcile within himself the demands of reason and conscience with his infirmity and his lack of strength, he once again turns to the preachers of salvation with the question, How can I be saved? How can I justify my inability to fulfill the conditions of salvation? And how about those who instruct —have they the strength resolutely to accomplish what they teach?

"Ask God; pray to God that He would help you!"

So the questioner concludes: Would it not have been more fruitful to have learned first of all that prayer is the source of all which Christian devotion demands and by which salvation is attained? And so he begins to study prayer. He reads, meditates, and analyzes the teachings of spiritual writers on this subject. And without a doubt he finds in them many clear thoughts, profound insights, and forceful expressions. One writer eloquently discourses on the necessity of prayer, another about its power and its benefits; also man's obligation to pray and the necessary conditions of prayer: fervor, attention, warmth of the spirit, purity of thought, reconciliation with enemies, humility, contrition, etc.

But what is the essence of prayer? And how does one actually pray? To this first and fundamental question one seldom finds a comprehensive and clear explanation, and consequently the man who seeks to learn the art of prayer finds himself once again under the veil of mystery. From general reading he gets ideas about the external acts of piety and concludes that to pray it is necessary to go to church, to make the sign of the cross, make prostrations, kneel, read the psalter, or recite the canons or afakists.

This is a common understanding of prayer of those who are not familiar with the writings of the Fathers about interior prayer and contemplation.

At last the aspirant encounters the book called *Philokalia*, in which twenty-five holy Fathers clearly explain the essence and the truth about prayer of the heart. Here the curtain is raised before the mystery of salvation and prayer, and he sees that really to pray means to direct the mind and heart to constant remembrance of God, to walk in His divine presence, to arouse in oneself the love of God by means of meditation, and to say the name of Jesus in harmony with one's breathing and the beating of one's heart. He begins this process by vocally calling on the holy name of Jesus Christ at all times, in all places, and in all occupations, without interruption.

But while these lucid truths enlighten his mind, open to him a path of learning and achievement in prayer, and convince him to apply himself to these wise directives without delay, he continues to encounter periodic difficulties until such time as an experienced director clarifies the mystery of prayer from the *Philokalia* completely and shows him that it is constancy in prayer which is the single most powerful means for attaining perfection of interior prayer and salvation. Constancy in prayer is the foundation or basis which supports a whole range of spiritual activity. As St. Simeon the New Theologian says, "He who prays ceaselessly by this one good joins all good."

And so in order to present the truth of this revelation in its fullness, the director develops it in the following way:

The first condition necessary for salvation is true faith. Holy Scripture says, "Now it is impossible to please God without faith" (Heb. 11:6). He who has no faith will be judged. But it is clear from Holy Scripture that man of himself cannot give birth to faith even as small as the mustard seed; faith does not originate in us but is the gift of God; and as a spiritual gift it is given by the Holy Spirit.

What must one do then? How does man reconcile his need of faith with the impossibility of acquiring it by himself? Again Holy Scripture points to the means and also gives us examples: "Ask and you will receive." The Apostles could not of themselves bring their faith to perfection, and so they prayed to Jesus Christ, "Lord, increase our faith." This is an example of obtaining faith, and from this we can see that faith is attained through prayer.

Other conditions necessary for salvation in addition to faith are good deeds or virtues, because "faith is dead if it is separated from good deeds." Man is justified by his deeds and not by faith alone. "But if you wish to enter into life, keep the commandments. . . . You must not kill. You must not commit adultery. You must not bring false witness. Honor your father and mother, and you must love your neighbor as yourself" (Matt. 19:17–19). And it is necessary to observe these commandments together, as the Apostle James teaches: "You see, if a man keeps the whole of the Law, except for one small point at which he fails, he is still guilty of breaking it all" (Jas. 2:10). And Paul the Apostle says the following about human weakness: "No one can be justified in the sight of God by keeping the Law" (Rom. 3:20). "The Law, of course, as we all know, is spiritual; but I am unspiritual; I have been sold as a slave to sin. I cannot understand my own behavior. I fail to carry out the things I want to do, and I find myself doing the very things I hate. In my inmost self I dearly love God's Law, but I can see that my body follows a different law that battles against the law which my reason dictates" (Rom. 7:14–15, 22–23). How then is it possible to do the works of the law when man in his weakness cannot be justified by observing the law?

Man finds this impossible only until such time as he asks for it, until he prays for it. "You don't have what you want because you don't pray for it" (Jas. 4:2). And Jesus Christ Himself says, "Cut off from me you can do nothing." And in regard to acting through Him He says, "Make your home in me as I make mine in you. He who abides in me bears much fruit" (John 15:4 and 5). Now to abide in Him means to be continuously aware of His presence, ceaselessly to ask in His name: "If you ask anything in my name, I will do it" (John 14:14). Thus the possibility of doing good works is realized through prayer! An example of this is seen in St. Paul himself, who prayed three times that a temptation be taken away from him; he got down on his knees before God the Father, begging for strength of the inner man, and he was directed to pray ceaselessly about all his needs. From what has been said above, it follows that the salvation of man depends on prayer, and therefore prayer is of primary importance; it is more necessary than anything else, for it animates man's faith and is the source of all virtues. In a word, with prayer all goes well and without it no good deed of Christian devotion can be accomplished. For this reason constancy and regularity apply to prayer exclusively; other virtues have their own time, but we are commanded to practice prayer without interruption; to pray constantly. It behooves us to pray always, at all times, and in all places.

True prayer must have its conditions; it is to be offered with a pure mind and heart, with ardent zeal, with undivided attention, with reverence and deepest humility. But who in good conscience does not admit that he is far from fulfilling these conditions for prayer, that he prays more out of necessity, by forcing himself, than by natural inclination, joyfully, and out of love of prayer? Sacred Scripture testifies to the fact that man does not have the strength to keep his spirit steadfast and to purify his mind from unseemly thoughts: "Man's heart contrives evil from his infancy." It is God alone who gives us a pure heart and a steadfast spirit, for "both the will and the action" are of God. And the Apostle Paul says, "My spirit may be praying but my mind is left barren" (1 Cor. 14:14). And, "We cannot choose words in order to pray properly" (Rom. 8:26). From this we can see that of ourselves we cannot fulfill the essential conditions of prayer.

What then can man do toward his salvation when his weakness is so great? He can acquire neither faith nor good works without prayer, and by his own power he cannot pray properly. What then is to be his contribution toward salvation, what is within the range of his freedom and his ability? Is there anything he can do so that he will not perish but be saved?

Every act has its perfection, but the Lord reserved this gift to His own will. So that man would see clearly his dependence on God's will and would learn real humility, God left to man's freedom and ability only the constant flow of prayer. God commands us to pray ceaselessly, at all times, and in all places. This is where the secret of true prayer, of faith, of keeping the commandments, and of salvation is found. Man has the ability to pray regularly and frequently. The Fathers of the Church clearly confirm this. St. Macarius the Great says, "To pray often is in our will, but to pray truly is a gift of grace." And Venerable Hesychius says that constancy in prayer becomes a habit which then turns into a natural state; he also says that without frequent calling on the name of Jesus Christ it is not possible to purify the heart. Venerable Callistus and Ignatius recommended frequent, uninterrupted prayer in the name of Jesus Christ before all actions and good works because constancy can bring even careless prayer to perfection. And Blessed Diadoch says emphatically that, if man would call on the name of the Lord as frequently as possible, then he would not fall into sin. How full of wisdom and experience these directives of the Fathers are, and how they warm the heart; their simplicity is the result of experience, and they shed light on the ways and methods of perfection.

What great contrast there is between their teaching and the moral directives of theoretical reason! Reason dictates: Do this and that good, arm yourself with manliness, use your will power, let the fruits of virtue persuade you, that is, purify your mind and heart of vain dreams, fill their place with instructive thoughts, do good, and you will be respected and at peace; live as your reason and conscience direct you. But alas! All this reasoning power will not reach its purpose without frequent prayer and its saving help. Let us look again at the teachings of the Fathers and see what they say, for example, about the cleansing of the soul. St. John Climacus writes that "when the soul is darkened by impure thoughts, you can overcome them by frequently calling on the name of Jesus. You will not find a more powerful and successful tool than this either in heaven or on earth." And St. Gregory says the following: "Know that no man can control his thoughts; therefore when impure thoughts come to the mind, call on the name of Jesus Christ frequently and the thoughts will of themselves quiet down." What a simple and practical method and born of experience! And what contrast with the theoretical directive, which attempts to reach purity by its own efforts. After considering these directives of the holy Fathers, tried by experience, we come to the conclusion that the primary and most conducive method for performing actions leading to salvation and spiritual perfection is constant, uninterrupted prayer, no matter how weak it is.

O Christian soul! If you do not find in yourself the strength to worship God in spirit and in truth; if your heart does not yet feel the warmth and sweetness of mental interior prayer, then bring to prayer that sacrifice which you can, which is in the power of your will and your strength. Let your lips first become familiar with frequent, uninterrupted prayerful calling; let them constantly, without interruption call on the powerful name of Jesus Christ. This does not require great effort and is possible for everyone. St. Paul, from his abundant experience, advocates this: "Through him, let us offer God an unending sacrifice of praise, a verbal sacrifice that is offered every time we acknowledge his name" (Heb. 13:15). Constancy in prayer will certainly become a habit and then second nature, and in time it will bring the mind and heart to a wholesome attitude. Imagine this: if a man would steadfastly observe this one precept of the Lord regarding prayer then by this one he would fulfill all the other precepts; because if he would pray in all places and at all times and in all occupations, if he would secretly call on the divine name of Jesus Christ, even if at the beginning without much fervor so that he had to force himself, he would then not have time for sinful sensual pleasures. Every sinful thought of his would meet opposition before it had a chance to develop; every sinful act would be considered less attractive than in an empty mind; useless talking would either be diminished or be completely eradicated, and every offense would immediately be purified by grace from the frequent calling on the name of the Lord. Constant exercise in prayer would draw the soul away from sinful actions and would bring it to essential knowledge and to union with God! Now do you see how important and necessary is constancy in prayer? It is the sole method of acquiring pure and true prayer, the best preparation for it, and the easiest way of reaching the goal in prayer and salvation!

To convince yourself even more of the necessity and fruitfulness of frequent prayer, (1) note carefully that every aspiration, every thought in prayer is the act of the Holy Spirit and the voice of your guardian angel, and (2) that the name of Jesus Christ called on in prayer contains within itself real, self-activating salutary power, and therefore (3) do not be disturbed by the impurity or dryness of your prayer, but with patience await the fruit resulting from frequent calling on the name of the Lord. Do not listen to the inexperienced, foolish suggestion of the world that though constant such prayer is only so many empty words. No! The power of the name of the Lord, if frequently called on, will bring its fruit in due time!

One spiritual writer describes this beautifully. "I know," he says, "that for many seemingly spiritual but pseudowise philosophers, seeking false grandeur and actions which seem noble in the eyes of reason and pride, the simple, vocal, and frequent exercise in prayer seems insignificant or useless. But they are unhappily mistaken in forgetting the precept of Jesus Christ: "I tell you solemnly, unless you change and become like little children you will never enter the kingdom of heaven" (Matt. 18:3). They fabricate for themselves a knowledge of prayer based on the unstable foundation of natural reason. Does it require much education, brains, or knowledge to say earnestly, "Jesus, Son of God, have mercy on me"? Was not this the kind of frequent prayer that the divine Teacher Himself praised? Was it not by such short but frequent words that miracles were performed? Ah, Christian soul! Take courage, and do not cease to call on the name of the Lord! Even if this cry comes from a heart which is distracted and filled with worldly concerns, do not worry! Only continue to recite the Prayer; do not become silent and do not lose your peace, for prayer will purify itself by repetition. Do not ever forget that "you have in you one who is greater than anyone in this world" (1 John 4:4). "God is greater than our conscience and knows everything," says the Apostle.

And so, after all these convincing reasons why constancy of prayer, despite human weakness, is so very powerful and is surely within the range of man's ability and his will, decide to experience it at least for one day in the beginning. Observe the constancy of your prayer so that calling on the name of Jesus Christ will receive more time than any other occupation; and this preference for prayer over worldly concerns will show you in time that this day was not lost but brought you closer to salvation; that on the scales of divine justice frequent prayer outweighs your weaknesses and actions and expiates the sins of that day in the book of life, places you on the path of righteousness, and gives you hope for attaining holiness and life eternal.

PILGRIM. With my whole heart I thank you, Reverend Father! You have comforted my sinful soul with this reading. For the sake of the Lord, please allow me to copy this article; I can do it in a couple of hours. All that you read is very beautiful and inspiring; it is as clear and precise for my dull mind as are the writings of the holy Fathers in the *Philokalia*. For example, John Carphatos in the fourth part of the *Philokalia* says that if you do not have strength for temperance and heroic deeds, then know that the Lord wishes to save you through prayer. And in your article this is so clearly developed. I thank God, and you, that I was worthy to hear this.

PROFESSOR. Highly esteemed Father, I also listened with great pleasure and attention. All the arguments are strictly logical and are remarkable. But it seems to me that the possibility of ceaseless prayer depends to a high degree on favorable circumstances, on quiet and solitude. I agree that frequent or ceaseless prayer is powerful and that it is the unique method of acquiring divine help in all acts of devotion and sanctification, and also that it is within the range of man's ability; but this method can be used only when man finds it possible to have silence and solitude. When he frees himself from work, from cares and entertainment, he can pray frequently and ceaselessly; then he only has to struggle with slothfulness or distracting thoughts. But if he is responsible for a job and is continuously busy and of necessity in the noisy company of other people, then no matter how earnestly he may wish to pray frequently, he will not be able to accomplish this because of inevitable distractions. Consequently, the unique method of frequent prayer requires favorable conditions and is therefore not suitable for everyone and is not meant for everyone.

MONK. Your conclusion serves no purpose. You do not mention the fact that the heart, accustomed to interior prayer, can pray at all times and by all occupations, both physical and mental; it can pray and call on the name of God without any difficulty in all kinds of noise. He who prays thus knows it from experience, and he who does not know it has to learn it gradually. It can be firmly stated that no form of external distraction can suppress prayer in him who wishes to pray, because the secret thought of man is not subject to any outward obligation and is absolutely free in itself. It can be controlled at all times and directed to prayer. And even the tongue can express the prayer secretly, without vocalizing it, around people and outward occupations.

Besides, our occupations are not so important and our conversations are not so engaging that one would find it impossible, in spite of them, periodically or even often, to call on the name of Jesus Christ—that is, if the mind is not yet accustomed to ceaseless prayer. But, of course, being alone and staying away from distracting involvements are necessary conditions for attentive and ceaseless prayer.

However, if it is not possible to have these, then we should not excuse ourselves for praying only seldom, for the quantity or constancy is possible for everyone; both for him who is sick and for him who is well. It depends on one's will. A proof of this can be seen in the examples of those who, though burdened with responsibilities, distracting obligations, work, cares, and anxieties, not only continuously called on the divine name of Jesus Christ but by this means learned and attained ceaseless interior prayer of the heart. Patriarch Photius was one of those. He was raised from a senator to the rank of a patriarch and, while directing a vast diocese in Constantinople, he ceaselessly called on the divine name and reached the goal of self-activating prayer of the heart. Callistus was another one who, though burdened with the responsibility of a cook on Mount Athos, learned ceaseless prayer. And the simplehearted Lazarus, overburdened with work for the brothers in a noisy atmosphere, calmed himself by continuously reciting the Jesus Prayer. There were many others who also called ceaselessly on the divine name.

If it were impossible to pray in distracting occupations or in the presence of other people, then, of course, we would not have been commanded to pray always. St. John Chrysostom says the following in his teaching about prayer: "No one can excuse himself from prayer under the pretext that he is occupied with daily cares or is not able to be in church. Everywhere, no matter where you find yourself, you can erect an altar to God in your heart by means of prayer." And so it is convenient to pray while traveling or at a market, trying to buy or sell something, or sitting behind one's trade; everywhere without exception it is possible to pray. Indeed, if a man makes an effort, then he will find it conducive to pray everywhere if he is convinced that prayer should take precedence over all his obligations and should constitute his main activity. This means, of course, that he will order his activities sensibly, that he will shorten his necessary conversations with people and will prefer silence to much useless talking. He could gain time for silent prayer by not being too preoccupied with superfluous cares. With such an approach, all of his activities would be marked by success by the power of the holy name. In time he would get accustomed to the uninterrupted calling on the name of Jesus Christ and would realize by experience that constancy in prayer, the unique method of salvation, is within man's capacity and his will. He would know that it is possible to pray at all times and under all circumstances, and gradually to pass from frequent vocal prayer to mental prayer and eventually to the Prayer of the heart and the realization that the kingdom of God is within.

PROFESSOR. I agree that it is possible and even convenient to practice frequent or uninterrupted prayer during mechanical work, because such work does not require deep concentration or much consideration and therefore my mind and lips can apply themselves to ceaseless prayer. But when I have to do something specifically mental, such as attentive reading or analyzing a profound subject or composing a literary piece, then how can I possibly pray both with my mind and lips? And as prayer is predominantly an act of the mind, how can I simultaneously give my mind to more than one activity?

MONK. We can answer your question easily if we take into consideration the fact that those who pray constantly can be divided into three groups: (1) the beginners, (2) those who have made some progress, and (3) those who have learned how to pray. The beginners can periodically raise their mind and heart to God and express a short vocal prayer even while they are engaged in mental work; and those who have made some progress in prayer or have attained certain recollection can do their intellectual work in constant awareness of God's presence, which is the basis of all prayer. This can be illustrated by the following example. Imagine that a very severe and exacting king commanded you to write an essay on some difficult subject in his very presence, at the feet of his throne. Now, no matter how completely engrossed you would be in your assignment, the presence of the king, who has authority over you and who has your life in his hands, would not allow you to forget even for a moment that you are not working alone, but that you are in a place which demands special reverence, respect, and propriety. This very real awareness of the presence of the king clearly illustrates the possibility of praying even while one is engaged in mental work.

And those who by long practice or by the grace of God have advanced from mental prayer to the Prayer of the heart pray not only when they are mentally occupied but even in their sleep. This truth is confirmed in the Song of Solomon: "I sleep but my heart is awake" (S. of S. 5:2). In those who have learned the art of prayer the heart calls on the name of the Lord with great ease; it rouses itself to prayer and draws both the mind and the soul into ceaseless prayerful outpouring regardless of the external circumstances or absorbing mental work of the one who prays.

PRIEST. Reverend Father, I also would like to express my thoughts. In the article which you read it was emphatically stated that the unique method of salvation and perfection is constancy in prayer, no matter how poor it is. This is not clear to me and I am wondering of what use is it to pray ceaselessly, to call on the name of the Lord with my tongue, when my attention is elsewhere and I am not aware of what I am saying? Is this not only useless repetition? The only result of this constant activity of the tongue will be a distraction for the mind and interference with its meditation. God asks not for words but for an attentive and pure heart. Is it not better to pray only rarely or at prescribed time but to say the short prayer with attention, fervor, warmth of the soul, and understanding? Otherwise, even if you pray day and night but without purity of soul and devotion, your prayer will be of no avail. You will recite a lot of words which will tire and bore you, and in the end your faith in prayer will weaken and you will give up this unfruitful exercise completely. Even Holy Scripture speaks forcefully about the uselessness of mere vocal prayer. "This people honors me only with lip-service, while their hearts are far from me" (Matt. 15:8). "It is not those who say to me, 'Lord, Lord,' who will enter the kingdom of heaven" (Matt. 7:21). "I would rather say five words that mean something than ten thousand words in a tongue" (1 Cor. 14:19). All of this points to the uselessness of merely external inattentive prayer of the lips.

MONK. Your conclusion would have some basis if the advice to pray vocally was not coupled with constancy or regularity; if the prayer in honor of the name of Jesus Christ did not have self-activating power and grow in attention and devotion as a result of constant repetition. But because the emphasis here is on constancy, on long duration, and ceaselessness in prayer, even if at the beginning it seems to lack attention or devotion, your conclusions do not hold.

Let us look at this in more detail. One spiritual writer, speaking forcefully about the power and fruitfulness of frequently repeating the same prayer, says in conclusion, "Many pseudoenlightened people regard this vocal and frequent practice of the same prayer useless and trivial, a mechanical and senseless occupation of simple people. But this mechanical exercise reveals a mystery of which they are, unfortunately, not aware. They do not realize that the vocal but frequent call is imperceptibly becoming a true cry of the heart, that it is becoming interiorized and as it were natural for the soul, that it enlightens and nourishes the soul and unites it with God."

It seems to me that those who criticize frequent vocal prayer can be compared to little children who are being taught how to read by learning the alphabet first. They become bored by this study and they complain, saying, "Is it not a hundred times better for us to go fishing like our fathers than to spend the day constantly repeating the ABCs or scribbling on paper with a quill pen?" The benefits, the enlightenment coming from reading which is the result of the repetition of letters is for them a mystery. In the same way there is a hidden mystery contained in the simple but frequent calling on the name of the Lord for those who have no knowledge and conviction of its end result. They measure an act of faith with the power of their inexperienced and nearsighted reason and forget that man consists of body and soul.

For what purpose, for example, when you wish to purify the soul do you first cleanse the body, impose a fast on yourself, and deprive your body of nourishing and stimulating food? Of course so that it would not prevent you from receiving, or rather that it would help you to achieve, purity of soul and enlightenment of the mind; that constant bodily hunger would remind you of your resolution to seek inner perfection and to practice virtue, which is so easy for you to forget. And you realize through experience that by means of the external fast of your body your reasoning powers become refined, you achieve a peace of heart and have a tool by which to control your passions and also a reminder of your spiritual efforts. And so by means of outward exercises you receive spiritual gifts. Constant vocal prayer is to be understood in a similar way, for by its repetition it develops inner prayer of the heart and promotes union with God.

It is foolish to imagine that by frequent repetition the lips become tired and that boredom, dryness, and lack of understanding necessitate giving up this outward prayerful exercise. No! Experience points to something quite contrary; those who practice ceaseless prayer convince us that the following happens: Once they have decided to call on the name of Jesus Christ constantly, to say the Jesus Prayer without interruption, they do of course experience difficulty at the beginning and struggle with slothfulness; but the more they practice the Prayer and for longer periods of time, the more they get used to this exercise, until gradually the lips and the tongue become self-activated and say the Prayer involuntarily. And even the muscles in the throat become so attuned to this exercise that he who prays finds the practice becoming very natural, and if he stops he immediately misses it. This is a sign that the mind is becoming attentive and is listening to this involuntary activity of the lips, which in the end becomes a source of delight and of true Prayer of the heart. This in fact is the real and beneficial result of frequent or ceaseless vocal prayer, very different from the conclusions of the inexperienced, who do not understand this activity!

And the scriptural references which you give as a proof of your objection can be clarified by careful analysis. Christ Jesus condemned hypocritical lip service or the mere call of "Lord, Lord," because the proud Pharisees had faith in God only on their lips and not in their hearts. This admonition was addressed to those who had no living faith, and it does not apply to the prayer which Christ strictly and definitely commanded in these words: "It behooves you to pray always and not to faint." Similarly St. Paul gives preference to five words uttered with understanding rather than a great deal of words said either without thought or in an unfamiliar tongue in church; this is to be understood as a general instruction and not specifically referring to prayer, of which he firmly says, "In every place, then, I want the men to lift their hands up reverently in prayer" (1 Tim. 2:8). And he also says, "Pray constantly" (1 Thess. 5:17).

Do you now see that simple but frequent prayer is most fruitful? And that careful analysis of Scripture is necessary for correct understanding?

PILGRIM. This is really true, Reverend Father! I have seen many who in all simplicity, without any instruction and not even knowing what attention is, practiced the Jesus Prayer vocally and ceaselessly and acquired the habit so that the tongue and lips said the prayer involuntarily, and in the end they experienced such delight and enlightenment that they were transformed from weak and negligent people into ascetics and heroes of virtue.

MONK. Yes! Prayer has the power to regenerate man. Its force is so great that no human passion or suffering can prevail against it. Before we part, I would like to read for you, if I may, a very brief but interesting article which I have with me.

ALL. We will gladly listen to it!

The Power of Prayer

Prayer is so dynamic and powerful that you can pray and do what you wish and prayer will bring you to the right and just action.

For a good and holy life pleasing to God nothing is as important as love. Love and do whatever you wish, says St. Augustine, because he who truly loves will not wish to do anything which is displeasing to his beloved. And because prayer is an act of outpouring love, this can be said of it also. Nothing is as necessary for salvation as regular prayer.

Pray and do what you wish, and you will reach the perfection of prayer and holiness and transformation.

For a thorough understanding of this we will illustrate it by examples.

1. Pray and think what you will, for your thoughts will be purified by prayer. Prayer will enlighten your mind, will quiet and disperse all your irrelevant thoughts. St. Gregory of Sinai confirms this when he says, "If you wish to drive away distracting thoughts and purify your mind, do so by prayer, for nothing else is capable of holding the mind more than prayer." And St. John Climacus says the following: "Conquer the enemies of thought through the name of Jesus, for you will not find a better tool than this."

2. Pray and do what you will, and your actions will become devout and fruitful and beneficial for your salvation. Frequent prayer, regardless for what intention, will not be without fruit, because it contains divine power, says Mark the Hermit. "All who call on the name of the Lord will be saved" (Acts 2:21). For example, a person praying without success and devotion received understanding and a call to repentance. A pleasure-seeking girl prayed for a change of heart, and prayer showed her the path to virginal life and gave her the strength to listen to the precepts of Jesus Christ.

3. Pray and do not try hard by your own power to overcome your passions. Prayer will destroy them in you. "You have in you one who is greater than anyone in this world" (1 John 4:4). And St. John Carpathos teaches that, if you do not have the gift of temperance, you should not be dejected but believe that God wishes you to apply yourself to prayer, and prayer will save you.

Another example of this is found in the *Lives of the Fathers*, where we read about an elder who fell into sin; he did not give in to despondency but turned to prayer and regained his peace.

4. Pray and do not be apprehensive about anything; do not be afraid of trouble or misfortune, for prayer will protect you and sustain you under all circumstances. Re-

member that Peter was drowning because of his lack of faith; remember Paul praying in prison and the monk who was freed from persistent temptation and the girl who was saved from an ill-intentioned soldier as a result of prayer and many other similar examples which all confirm the power, efficacy, and universality of prayer uttered in the name of Jesus Christ.

5. Pray always, no matter how poorly, and do not be disturbed by anything; be happy in spirit and at peace, for prayer will direct your life and give you understanding. Remember what the saints say about the power of prayer. St. John Chrysostom confirms that "prayer, though coming from us full of sin, is immediately purified." And Mark the Hermit says, "To make an effort to pray is in our power, but to pray purely is a gift of grace." And so offer to God what is in your power. Begin by bringing to God a sacrifice of constancy in prayer, and God's almighty power will swallow your weakness; your dry and distracted but frequent prayer will become a habit and second nature; your prayer will be made pure, fervent, and powerful.

6. And finally, if you will use all your time to pray, then naturally you will not have time left either for sinful deeds or even for sinful thoughts.

Do you see now what depth there is in that wise saying: "Love and do what you will, pray and do what you wish?" How comforting and encouraging this is for the sinner who is weighed down with weakness and is groaning under the load of his warring passions.

Prayer, then, is the all-embracing means for reaching salvation and perfection. Yes, but prayer is coupled with a condition, for Scripture commands that we pray *always*. Consequently only frequent and uninterrupted prayer is very effective and powerful. And we know that constancy is within our will power, just as purity, fervor, and perfection of prayer are a gift of grace.

And so we will pray as often as possible; we will consecrate our whole life to prayer even if at the beginning it is distracted; constancy will teach us attention, and quantity will definitely lead to quality. One experienced spiritual writer has said that to learn to do anything well it is necessary to do it as often as possible.

PROFESSOR. Prayer is truly a great activity! And zeal in being constant in it is the key which opens its blessed treasures. But how frequently there is an inner struggle within me between zeal and slothfulness! How wonderful it would be to find a means which would help me resolutely, convincingly, and wholeheartedly give myself to ceaseless prayer.

MONK. Spiritual writers enumerate a variety of methods, based on sound principles, which can awaken one to diligence in prayer. For example, they suggest (1) that we deepen our conviction about the necessity of prayer and its effectiveness and fruitfulness toward salvation; (2) that we should firmly convince ourselves of God's unconditional command to pray and that Scripture reminds us of this obligation; (3) that we should always remember how impossible it is to succeed in acts of devotion and attain peace and salvation without frequent prayer and that we must answer for negligence in prayer both here on earth and in the life to come; and (4) that we strengthen our resolution with the examples of the servants of God who by this means of ceaseless prayer attained salvation and holiness.

Now all of these methods are sound and are based on true understanding of prayer. However, the pleasure-loving and spiritually sick soul does not profit fully by these suggestions even when it is aware of them, for on the one hand they are a bitter medicine for its indulged taste and on the other they are not strong enough for the deeply damaged human nature. Is there a Christian who does not know that it is necessary to pray often and diligently and that God commands this, that for slothfulness toward God we will have to suffer punishment, and that all the saints prayed ardently and constantly? However, all this knowledge seldom shows its beneficial results! Everyone can observe in himself that he does not live up to these directions of reason and conscience and that in failing to do so he lives very poorly and slothfully.

Therefore, the holy Fathers, who in their wisdom and experience are fully aware of the weakness of man's will and his greediness for pleasure, like wise physicians prescribe bitter medicine coated with sugar. They show a very easy method, consisting of prayer and trust in God's help, to destroy slothfulness and negligence in prayer and to attain perfection and love of God. They encourage us to think as much as possible about such a blessed state of the soul and to read about it in the writings of the Fathers, who reassure us how easy it is to attain the joys of interior prayer and how wonderful they are. The sweetness of the heart, warmth and light, unspeakable rapture, joy, ease, profound peace, blessedness, and love of life are all the result of prayer of the heart. When we immerse ourselves in meditation about such things, our weak and tepid soul is warmed, strengthened, and encouraged toward success in prayer and is, as it were, enticed to test the exercise of prayer. St. Isaac of Syria says, "Joy, which is an enticement to the soul, is the result of hope which has blossomed; and meditation on one's hope brings contentment to the heart." And he continues, "From the beginning of this activity to the end some form of success is presupposed; there is hope of seeing it realized. This encourages the mind to direct its action to this goal and consequently to find joy in this activity." Venerable Hesychius, in writing about slothfulness and negligence in prayer, as well as the realization of the need to renew one's zeal to continue to pray, says, "We wish to be in solitude for no other reason than the sweetness and joy which it brings to the soul." And from this it follows that this Father presents joy and delight as the rewards for zeal in prayer. Macarius the Great teaches that "our spiritual efforts or prayer should be done with the goal and hope of enjoying the fruits of prayer in our hearts." Many clear examples of this powerful method are seen throughout the *Philokalia* where the delights of prayer are described; they should be read as often as possible by the one who struggles with the enemy of slothfulness or aridity in prayer. However, he should consider himself unworthy of these delights and constantly reproach himself for his negligence in prayer.

PRIEST. Will this kind of thinking not lead the inexperienced to what the theologians call spiritual gluttony, an attitude of the soul which is greedy for excessive consolations and gifts of grace, and, instead of being satisfied with fulfilling the act of devotion as a duty and a debt, dreams about a reward?

PROFESSOR. I think that the theologians caution against excessive greediness for spiritual consolations, but they do not completely disapprove of seeking sweetness and consolation in virtue. It is true that to wish a reward is not the most perfect intention for doing good, but it is not against God's will, for He Himself promises us a reward if we keep the commandments and attain perfection. "Honor your father and your mother," is a commandment, and the promise of its reward follows immediately: "so that you may have long life and may prosper" (Deut. 5:16). "If you wish to be perfect, go and sell what you own and give the money to the poor," is a demand for perfection, and the reward follows immediately: "and you will have treasure in heaven" (Matt. 19:21). "Happy are you when people hate you, drive you out, abuse you, denounce your name as criminal, on account of the Son of Man." Here is a great demand for discipline requiring tremendous strength of spirit and heroic patience, and for such effort there is a great reward and comfort for those who can fulfill it: "Rejoice when that day comes and dance for joy, for then your reward will be great in heaven" (Luke 6:22–23). Therefore, I think that some desire for consolation in the prayer of the heart is necessary and is really the chief means of encouraging success and diligence. This clearly confirms the practical instructions of our brother monk which we have just heard.

MONK. A great theologian, Macarius of Egypt, speaks very clearly about this: "As in planting an orchard diligence and effort is exerted with the hope of receiving fruit—and if there is no fruit, all the effort will have been in vain—so in prayer, if you don't find in yourself the spiritual fruits of love, peace, joy, etc., your effort will be useless. Therefore, the goal of our spiritual efforts should be consolation and sweetness in our hearts." Do you see how clearly this Father resolved the question of the necessity of consolation in prayer? And I recall a thought on this from one spiritual writer that it is very natural for man to pray, that there is in him an innate desire to give himself in worship. Now consideration of this innate quality can serve as a strong incentive for arousing diligence in prayer, the means that the professor is so eagerly waiting for. I will tell you briefly what I remember from this article. This spiritual author writes that nature and reason lead man to the knowledge of God. Reason examines the fact that there can be no action without a cause, and that there is a chain of causation going from lower to higher beings and finally coming to the highest cause, or God. And nature shows astonishing wisdom in every aspect of creation as well as harmony, order, and gradation and gives the basic material for the ascending ladder going from finite causes to the infinite. In this way man can come to the knowledge of God naturally. And for this reason there never was a nation or a people who were without some knowledge of God. The result of this knowledge is that primitive man without any exterior prompting, as it were involuntarily, directs his gaze toward heaven, falls on his knees, and utters an incomprehensible but necessary sigh; he feels spontaneously that something is drawing him to the heights, that something unknown compels him. From this inner knowledge arise all the natural religions, and what is extraordinary is that the essence of every religion consists in some form of prayer, expressing itself in some form of movement of the spirit and outward sacrifice, though it is more or less distorted by ignorance and superstition of pagan people. The more surprising this reality is in the eyes of reason, the more it demands an understanding of this mystery which is recognized in man's natural inclination toward prayer.

The psychological answer to this is not difficult to find. The root, the head, and power of all passions and actions of man is innate self-love. This is clearly confirmed in man's tendency toward self-preservation. Every desire, every undertaking, every action of man has as its goal self-fulfillment and happiness. The natural tendency of man is to be preoccupied with self-fulfillment throughout his whole life. But the spirit of man is not satisfied with anything sensual, and innate self-love never quiets down in its aspiration. Therefore, the desires are developed more and more, the longing for happiness grows and fills the imagination and attunes the emotions to this. The outpouring of this inner feeling and desire of itself inclines one toward prayer, but because of self-love it reaches its goal with difficulty. The less man succeeds in attaining happiness, the more he has his mind set on it; the more he desires it, the more urgently he pours out his desire in prayer. He ardently asks the Cause of all being for what he needs. And so innate self-love, the chief element of life, is the basic reason which arouses the natural man to prayer.

In wisdom, the Creator poured into the human nature of man the capacity for self-love as an enticement, as the Fathers would say, which would attract the fallen human being to heavenly aspiration.

Oh, if man would not corrupt this capacity but would preserve it in its excellence united with his spiritual nature! Then he would have strong encouragement and means on the way to moral perfection. But alas! How often in this noble capacity he gives in to the passion of self-love when he turns it into the instrument of his lower nature.

ELDER. My dear guests, I thank you wholeheartedly. Your conversation was most inspiring and greatly comforted and instructed me in my limited experience. May the Lord bless you and give you His grace for your edifying example.

All part.

CHAPTER 7

Pray for one another and this will cure you. (Jas. 5:16)

PILGRIM. My devout companion, the professor, and I felt compelled to stop by to say good-bye and to ask you to pray for us before we start on our journey.

PROFESSOR. Yes, we are grateful for your hospitality and the spiritual discussion which we enjoyed with you and your friends. The memory of this will stay in our hearts as a reminder of our sharing in Christian love in the distant land to which we are destined.

ELDER. Thank you for remembering me and also for your timely visit. I have two traveling guests: a Moldavian monk and a hermit who has lived in the forest in solitude for twenty years. They would like to meet you and I will call them immediately.

Here they are!

PILGRIM. Oh, how peaceful is the life in the desert! How conducive and easy to raise one's soul to union with God! The silent forest is like the garden of Eden, in which the sweet tree of life grows in the prayerful heart of the desert-dweller. If I knew a way of feeding myself, I would choose that life style above all others.

PROFESSOR. Everything looks exceptionally attractive from a distance, but we know from experience that every place has its advantages and also its disadvantages. Of course, to a person who has a melancholy temperament and a natural inclination for silence, the life of a hermit seems attractive; but what dangers one is faced with on that path! The history of ascetical life gives many examples of hermits and recluses who, as a result of complete alienation from people, fell into self-deception and delusion.

HERMIT. I am surprised to note how frequently one hears in Russia, not only in monasteries but also from some God-fearing laymen, that many who desire ascetical life or wish to practice interior prayer are kept from following this inclination because of fear that they will perish from self-deception. They insist on this and give examples to substantiate their claims; in reality they are strangers to interior life, so they estrange others from it also. I think that there are two reasons for this: either from misunderstanding of interior life and lack of spiritual enlightenment, or from personal indifference to contemplation and envy lest others who seem to be less enlightened than they should pass them up. It is very unfortunate that those who hold such convictions do not examine the discourses of the holy Fathers on this subject, for they teach truly and resolutely that there is no need to fear or doubt when one calls on God for help. And if some of the hermits did, indeed, fall into self-deception or fanaticism, it was the result of pride; they did not have a director and mistook their visions and dreams for reality. If such a trial would occur, it would bring experience and a crown of glory because God's unfailing help is there to protect the one who is being tested. "Courage! It is I! Do not be afraid," says the Lord Jesus. From this it follows that fear and apprehension of interior life because of the possibility of self-deception is useless; humble acknowledgment of one's sins, openness of one's soul to a director, and imageless prayer are a stronghold against deception which so many greatly fear and because of which they do not aspire to contemplation. However, those who fear contemplative action are in reality the ones who are deceived, according to the wise words of Philoteus of Sinai, who says the following: "Many of the monks do not recognize the delusion of their own mind which comes to them from the devil; they apply themselves diligently to external acts of virtue but completely neglect interior contemplation because they lack knowledge and enlightenment." And Gregory of Sinai says, "Even if they hear about it from others who have experienced interior delight, out of envy they consider this self-deception."

PROFESSOR. Please allow me to ask you a couple of questions. Of course that acknowledgment of one's sins is necessary for everyone who takes his spiritual life seriously, but how is one to proceed in the event that there is no experienced director who could lead him on the interior path, hear his confession, and give him accurate and trustworthy guidance in spiritual life? In such a case is it better then not to consider contemplative life at all rather than attempt it without a director? Also, I do not understand how it is possible to place oneself in the presence of God and safeguard imageless prayer absolutely. This is not natural, because our soul or mind cannot present anything in the imagination without a form, in absolute formlessness. And why when one's mind is immersed in God cannot one imagine or visualize Jesus Christ, the Blessed Trinity, etc.?

HERMIT. One of the chief conditions for living in solitude and learning the prayer of the heart is to have a wise and experienced spiritual director to whom one can go regularly and with confidence open his heart and share his thoughts and all that he has encountered on the path of interior knowledge. However, if it is not possible to find such a guide, the holy Fathers recommend an alternative. Here is what Nicephorus the Monk clearly teaches in this regard: "In the practice of the interior activity of the heart it is necessary to have an experienced director. If one is not available, you should diligently search for one. If, however, you cannot find one, with a humble and contrite heart call on God to help you to apply the precepts and direction of the teachings of the Fathers and to verify this with the word of God as given in Holy Scripture." In this regard, it is also important to keep in mind that he who is sincere in his spiritual search will recognize true instruction even when it comes from simple, ordinary people. The Fathers say that if with faith and the right attitude you ask even a Saracen, you can gain valuable insights; but without faith and the right intention, even if you ask a prophet for direction, you will not be satisfied. We see an example of this in Macarius the Great of Egypt, who once received instruction from a simple peasant which enabled him to overcome his difficulties.

Now let us look at your question of imageless prayer—what it is and why the holy Fathers so strongly advocate it. During the time of contemplation one is to avoid every kind of dreaming and is not to imagine or receive any kind of vision of light, of a saint, an angel, or of Christ. The Fathers warn strongly about this because the power of imagination could easily personify the ideas of the mind and the inexperienced could be lured by these images, regard them as visions of grace, and so give in to self-deception. Holy Scripture confirms this warning when it says that the devil can come to us as an angel of light. Now it is possible for the mind, while in the presence of God, naturally and easily to sustain and safeguard imageless prayer. The power of the mind can perceive and hold its attention on an idea which has no concrete and visible form. For example, you can be aware of your soul, of air, of warmth and cold; when you are cold, you can have an idea of warmth which has no form or shape. In a similar way, it is possible to be aware of God's incomprehensible presence in a purely abstract way.

PILGRIM. In my wanderings I also came across pious people who claimed that they were afraid to attempt interior prayer because of delusion. For the benefit of some of them I read parts of the *Philokalia*, the precepts of St. Gregory of Sinai, who says that "the activity of the heart cannot be a delusion, because even if the enemy would wish to change the warmth of the heart into violent burning, or change the joys of the heart into sensual pleasure, time, experience, and the feeling itself would manifest the enemy's craftiness even to those who are not very familiar with his tricks." Unfortunately, I also met those who were on the path of silence and prayer of the heart but because of some stumbling block or a sinful weakness they gave into dejection and abandoned interior activity of the heart.

PROFESSOR. Yes, that is very natural! I myself sometimes experience this when I become distracted or am guilty of some sin. Since the interior prayer of the heart is a holy activity, and oneness with God, is it proper to practice a holy activity in a sinful heart, and not purify it first in silent and humble repentance and sufficient preparation for union with God? It is better to be mute before God than to offer inattentive prayer from a sinful and distracted heart.

MONK. It is unfortunate that you draw such a conclusion! Dejection is worse than any other kind of sin and is the strongest instrument which the world of darkness uses against us. Out of the abundance of their experience the holy Fathers give us a teaching on this which is quite contrary to your conclusion. The venerable Nikita Stethatus says, even if you fall into the depths of infernal evil, do not despair but turn quickly to God and He will soon raise your sinful heart and will give you more strength than you had before. And so after every fall and sinful wound of the heart you should promptly place yourself in the presence of God to be healed and purified. This can be compared to placing spoiled things in the sun and allowing the rays of the sun to kill the contagion and the pungent odor. Many spiritual Fathers speak forcefully about this. In the struggle with our passions, the enemies of salvation, we should never give up our life-giving activity of calling on the Lord Jesus present in our hearts! Our sinful actions should not prevent us from walking in the presence of God and from interior prayer, arousing disharmony, dejection, and sorrow, but should prompt us to turn quickly to God. An infant who is learning to walk will look to his mother and will hold on to her even more tightly when he stumbles.

HERMIT. I think that the main cause of dejection and of disturbing thoughts of doubt is a distracted mind which does not keep watch over its silent dwelling. The ancient and wise Fathers succeeded in overcoming dejection and received enlightenment; their main source of strength was their trust in God and their peaceful solitude. Their salutary advice to us is: "Sit silently in your cell and it will teach you everything."

PROFESSOR. I respect your judgment and find your critical analysis of my thoughts most interesting. However, I would like to comment on your praise of silence and the great benefit of seclusion which the hermits love. This is how I see the matter: In the natural order of things God ordained that human beings necessarily depend on one another; they are responsible for one another and all through life they are to work for one another and sustain one another. The welfare of mankind and love of neighbor is based on this social aspect. But how can the silent recluse who alienates himself from people serve his neighbor in his inactivity, or what contribution does he bring to the welfare of human society? He really destroys in himself the order of the Creator regarding love of neighbor and the beneficial influence he should have on his fellow man.

HERMIT. Inasmuch as your idea of silence is erroneous, your conclusion is also incorrect. Let us look at this in detail.

1. The person who lives in solitude is not idle; he is even more active than the individual who lives in society, but the hermit's activity is of a higher order. He works untiringly on a higher plane as he observes, analyzes, and evaluates the state of his moral existence. This is the true goal of silence! And to the degree that this is beneficial for his own perfection, it is also beneficial for his neighbor who does not have the opportunity to live in solitude and be specifically concerned with his moral growth. The real hermit shares his interior experiences by passing them on either in writing or, in exceptional cases, vocally, and in this way he assists his fellow men spiritually in their work of salvation. His service has greater value than that of a secular philanthropist, whose benefits are conferred on a small number of people. For he who teaches moral values and shares his spiritual riches serves a whole nation. His experiences and instructions pass on from one generation to another, as we can readily see by what we are using from ancient times. These charitable acts of mercy done for the sake of Christ are a service of the highest order, for Christian love surpasses all.

2. The positive and salutary influence of the hermit on his neighbor can be seen not only in what he shares of wisdom and experience regarding interior life, but his life of renunciation is itself an example to the attentive layman and can inspire him to self-knowledge and devotion. When a secular person hears about a devout hermit, or passes by his hermitage, he experiences a desire for a devout life and he thinks how man on earth can return to the original contemplative state with which he came from the hands of the Creator. The silent hermit teaches by his silence; he benefits others with his very life and edifies and encourages others to seek God.

3. The above-mentioned benefits come from a true hermit who has been enlightened and illumined with God's light. But if the hermit does not have the gifts of grace to be a light to the world and is in solitude only because of his slothfulness and negligence in associating with his fellow men, even then he can do a great service to society in not leading others to temptation by his bad example, just as the gardener cuts off the dry and unfruitful branches and pulls out the weeds so that the good plants would grow unhindered.

St. Isaac of Syria speaks of the importance of solitude in this way: "If we place all the actions of our life on one side of the scale and silence on the other, we find that silence outweighs them all. Working signs and miracles in the world cannot be compared with the excellence of silence. Love the passivity of silence more than feeding the hungry of the world or converting many nations to God. It is better for you to free yourself from the bonds of sin than to free slaves from bondage."

Even the ancient philosophers knew the value of silence. The philosophical school of Neoplatonism, which under the leadership of Plotinus had many followers, strongly emphasized contemplative interior life which could be realized in silence. One spiritual writer said that even if the state were developed to the highest degree in education and morality, in addition to secular activities there would be a need for people with contemplative goals to preserve the spirit of truth, to receive it from past ages, and to pass it on to posterity. Such people in the Church are the hermits, recluses, and solitaries.

PILGRIM. It seems to me that no one praised the value of silence more than St. John Climacus, who says, "Silence is the mother of prayer; it returns the sinner from the bondage of sin and imperceptibly leads him to success in virtue and closer to heaven." And Jesus Christ Himself showed us the value of solitude by frequently leaving his public ministry and going into the hills to pray in peace and quiet.

The contemplative hermits are the pillars of the Church, who by their ceaseless prayer support its piety. And even in ancient times there were many devout laymen and even kings and their dignitaries who went to see the hermits to ask for their prayers and guidance. Therefore, the silent hermit, by his life of prayer, can serve his neighbor and have a wholesome effect on him.

PROFESSOR. I must admit that I have a problem with this idea of asking others to pray for us. We Christians have the habit of asking others to pray for us, especially those whom we consider to be worthy members of the Church. But is this not simply an act of self-love, or copying the habit from others without giving the matter much thought? Does God really need a human intercessor? Does He not know everything and direct everything according to His providence and not according to our wishes? Does He not determine all before our petitions are uttered, as the Holy Scripture confirms? And can the prayer of many change God's purpose more than the prayer of one? Would not God be partial if that were so? And can the prayer of another save me when everyone is either approved or condemned for his own actions? Therefore, asking for the prayers of others is, in my opinion, nothing more than religious courtesy, a desire to please another or show him respect, and nothing else!

MONK. A merely superficial reasoning or secular philosophy could arrive at such an understanding, but spiritual reason, illumined by the light of religion and taught by the experience of interior life, penetrates things deeper, sees them in their true light, and arrives at an entirely different con-

clusion than that which you have presented! In order to
understand this more clearly and quickly, let us explain it by
means of an example and then confirm this truth by the
word of God.

Imagine a student going to a teacher for instruction, but
his limited ability as well as slothfulness and lack of discipline
prevents him from attaining success in his studies and he is
labeled a failure. This fact makes him very unhappy, but he
does not know what to do, how to overcome his difficulties.
Then he meets another student, a classmate of his who is
more capable than he, more diligent and successful, and he
tells him of his difficulties. The classmate responds by suggest-
ing that they study together and says to him, "We will study
together and it will be easier, more pleasant, and even more
beneficial for both of us." And so they begin to study together, sharing with one another what each understands of
the subject which they are studying in common. And what is
the outcome? After some time the negligent student becomes diligent, he begins to enjoy his studies, he becomes
zealous, and he understands what he is doing; and all of this
has a beneficial effect even on his character and his morality.
And his gifted friend becomes even more industrious and successful. They work and co-operate together and are both
richer for it.

Now this is a very natural thing because man is by nature a
social being and he develops his intellectual capacities
through others. His habits in life, his attitudes, feelings, and
aspirations, and everything he does is the result of his association with others. Because people have such a strong influence
upon one another, to live with a certain group of people
means to emulate their habits, activities, and even their morality. Consequently, the indifferent individual can become
enthusiastic, the dull one can become sharp, the slothful one
energetic simply by associating with men who have those positive qualities. The spirit of one can be given to another. One
can be inspired to prayer, to attention, or be encouraged
when he is dejected, diverted from vice and directed toward
wholesome activity. Helping one another in this way, men

can become more devout and enthusiastic and do things with greater ease. Here then is the reason for the common practice of Christians asking for prayer of one another, asking to be remembered by their brothers.

From this we can see that it is not that God is appeased with many petitions and intercessions, as is the case with the powerful on earth, but the spirit and the power of prayer purifies and enlightens the soul for whom prayers are being offered and prepares it for union with God.

If the mutual prayer of those who are living on earth is so fruitful, then it is obvious that prayer for those who passed on is also beneficial because of the close union which exists between the world of the spirit and this earth. It is therefore possible for the souls of the Church Militant to be in communion with those of the Church Triumphant or those who have departed.

Now everything which I have said thus far is based on psychological reasoning, but if we open the Holy Scripture we can find proof of this truth. Christ Jesus said to the apostle Peter, "But I have prayed for you, Simon, that your faith may not fail, and once you have recovered, you in your turn must strengthen your brothers" (Luke 22:32). Here the power of the prayer of Jesus Christ strengthens the spirit of Peter and sustains his faith in temptation. When the apostle Peter was in prison, prayer was being offered for him: "All the time Peter was under guard the Church prayed to God for him unremittingly" (Acts 12:5). Here we can see that prayer can help when our brethren are in unfortunate circumstances. But the clearest precept about prayer for our neighbor is expressed by the apostle James in these words: "So confess your sins to one another, and pray for one another, and this will cure you" (Jas. 5:16). The prayer uttered by the just will be very beneficial. This then definitely confirms the psychological conclusion which we have drawn above.

And what should we say about the teaching of the Apostle Paul, who gives us an example of asking others to pray? One writer points out that this example of St. Paul is supposed to teach us how necessary mutual prayer for one another is, when even so holy and courageous an ascetic acknowledges a need for spiritual help through the prayer of others. In his letter to the Hebrews Paul expresses his petition in this way: "We are sure that our own conscience is clear and we are certainly determined to behave honorably in everything we do; pray for us" (Heb. 13:18). When we see such an attitude, how unreasonable it would be for us to depend on our own prayer and accomplishments alone when so holy a man humbly asks his neighbors, the Hebrews, to unite their prayer to his own. And therefore, with humility, simplicity, and charity we should welcome and appreciate the prayers even of our brethren who are weak in faith, for the magnanimous spirit of the Apostle Paul did not discriminate but asked for common prayer of all. The power of God is shown in weakness and can sometimes be made perfect in the one who is praying. With this forceful example in mind, let us note that mutual prayer for one another nourishes Christian love and unity which God commands; it witnesses to the humility of the one who asks for prayer and to the spirit of the one who prays, and thus mutual prayer is nourished.

PROFESSOR. Your analysis is both beautiful and precise, but I would like to hear your comments on the method or form of prayer for our neighbor. I am thinking that if the fruitfulness and the effects of prayer depend on a real concern toward the neighbor, and specifically on the constant influence of the spirit of the one who prays on the spirit of the one who needs the prayer, then won't such an attitude of the soul distract one from the constant presence of God and the outpouring of the soul before God in its real need? And if one remembers to ask for God's help for one's neighbor only once or twice a day, will this be sufficient to help and stengthen the person one is praying for? In short, I would like to know what is the best method of praying for one's neighbor.

MONK. No matter what is the intention of the prayer brought before God, it need not and really cannot take you away from the presence of God, because if it is presented to God then it is, of course, in His presence. And regarding the method of prayer for one's neighbor I think that it is important to keep in mind that the power of this prayer depends on sincere Christian concern for one's neighbor, and the degree of influence on his soul depends on this. When you remember your neighbor or if you have a set time of prayer for him, you can use the following form: "Merciful Lord, may your will be done; you wish that all men come to the truth and be saved, have mercy and save your servant N. Receive this petition from me, as a cry of love which you have commanded." This form can be repeated whenever you are inspired to pray or you can use your rosary to pray for your neighbor.

PROFESSOR. I feel obliged to remember this inspiring and instructive conversation with all your views and ideas, and I thank you wholeheartedly for it.

PILGRIM AND PROFESSOR. And so the time for our departure has come; we earnestly ask for your prayers for our journey.

ELDER. "I pray that the God of peace, who brought our Lord Jesus Christ back from the dead to become the great Shepherd of the sheep by the blood that sealed an eternal covenant, may make you ready to do his will in any kind of good action; and turn us all into whatever is acceptable to himself through Jesus Christ, to whom be glory for ever and ever. Amen" (Heb. 13:20–21).

APPENDIX

St. Simeon the New Theologian

Interior prayer is truly marvelous but it is difficult to explain. For those without practical experience it seems not only incomprehensible but incredible. In fact, this form of prayer is very rare in our times because the snares of the devil entrap man in all forms of distraction and pure prayer can only be offered to God when the mind is free from all distracting thoughts.

The following conditions are necessary for success in this form of prayer: perfect obedience; guarding the purity of one's conscience in regard to God, to neighbor, and to objects; and a resolve to walk in the presence of God. If you proceed in this manner, you will prepare for yourself a direct path for interior prayer.

Your mind should guard your heart in time of prayer; the mind should constantly descend into the heart and from the depths of the heart offer up prayer to God.

You should do all this until such time as you taste the sweetness of the Lord. When finally the mind is in the heart and it tastes how sweet the Lord is, then it will not wish to leave the heart but will say with St. Peter, "Lord, it is wonderful for us to be here" (Matt. 17:4); then the mind will constantly look into the heart, and if it wanders, it will return there again and again and will repel the thoughts brought by the devil.

For those who have no knowledge and understanding of this inner activity it will seem difficult and oppressive. But those who have tasted the sweetness of the Lord in prayer will cry with St. Paul, "Nothing therefore can come between us and the love of Christ" (Rom. 8:35).

Therefore, our holy Fathers, who heard from the Lord that "from the heart come evil intentions: murder, adultery, fornication, theft, perjury, slander. These are the things that make a man unclean" (Matt. 15:19–20), also heard in another part of the Gospel that we should "clean the inside of the cup and dish first so that the outside may become clean as well" (Matt. 23:26). The Fathers abandoned every other spiritual pursuit and began wholeheartedly to practice this one activity, the guarding of the heart, for they were convinced that through this holy occupation they would easily attain every virtue but without it they would not attain any. This was their predominant occupation and they also wrote about it. He who wishes should read the writings of Mark the Hermit, St. Climacus, Hesychius of Jerusalem, Philotheus of Sinai, Abba Isaiah, Barsanuphius the Great, and others.

If you wish to learn how to descend into the heart and remain there I will tell you.

First you must observe the following three conditions: You must be free from all cares, not only from vain and unholy cares but even from good things. In other words, you should be dead to everything; your conscience should be pure and it should not denounce you in anything. You should be completely free from passionate attachments; your thoughts should not be inclined toward anything worldly. Then sit alone in a quiet place, close the door, take your mind from every temporal and vain thing, bow your head toward your chest and stay attentively inside of yourself, not in the head but in the heart, and holding the mind there with your inner eyes watch your breathing. With your mind find the place of the heart and let it abide there. In the beginning you will experience darkness and discomfort, but if you will continue this activity of attention without interruption, you will attain unceasing joy. If the mind continues with this activity, it will find the place of the heart and will see things it never knew and saw before. Then, no matter what distracting thoughts would come, it will immediately repel and destroy them through the name of Jesus. From this time also the mind will experience anger toward the demons and will pursue and overcome them. In addition what usually follows from this you will learn by experience if with the help of God you will guard your attention and keep your mind on the prayer "Lord Jesus Christ, have mercy on me!"

St. Gregory of Sinai

Having received the spirit of Jesus Christ by means of a pure prayer of the heart, we should communicate mystically with the Lord. But not understanding the greatness, honor, and glory resulting from grace and not caring about our spiritual growth through the keeping of the commandments and reaching true contemplation, we are careless and therefore fall into sensual habits and we throw ourselves into the abyss of insensitivity and darkness. It happens also that we think very little of God's presence and do not realize that we should be as rays of grace. We believe but not with a living faith, and despite the new spirit which we have received in baptism, we do not cease to live according to the flesh. If we do repent and begin to keep the commandments, we keep only the letter of the law and not the spirit and we are so alienated from spiritual life that even when we see it in others we imagine it as error and confusion. In this way we are dead in the spirit, alive but not in Christ and not in accordance with the conviction that what is born of the spirit should be spiritual.

However, what we have received in holy baptism of the life of Jesus Christ is not destroyed but is only buried as some treasure in the earth. But wisdom and grace demand a concern about this in order to reveal it and bring it into the open. But how?

Two methods can lead us to this actualization: In the first place, this gift is open to the one who keeps the commandments; and to the degree that we keep the commandments, we experience light and wisdom. In the second place, the method by which we can acquire this gift is ceaseless calling on the Lord Jesus or constant awareness of God's presence. The first means is powerful, but the second is even more powerful and it supports the first. Therefore, if we sincerely wish to reveal the abundance of grace buried in us, we will hasten to acquire the habit of the second method, the prayer of the heart, and we will practice this imageless activity until it warms our heart and enflames it to unspeakable love for the Lord.

The action of this prayer in the heart can be present in two ways: Sometimes the mind anticipates and attaches itself to the Lord in the heart by continual remembrance; at other times the prayer comes first in sparks of joy, attracts the mind to the heart, and binds it to call on the Lord Jesus in reverential presence before Him. In the first case the action of the prayer can be noticed in the subduing of the passions through the keeping of the commandments and the warmth of the heart which results from diligent calling on the Lord Jesus; in the second case the spirit attracts the mind to the heart and holds it there in the depths, keeping it from its usual wandering. From these two aspects of prayer the mind is either active or contemplative; when active it overcomes the passions with the help of God, and when contemplative it sees God as much as it is possible for a man to do.

The active prayer of the heart and mind can be accomplished in the following way: Sitting on a chair, bring your mind from the head into the heart and hold it there; from there call with your mind and heart, "Lord Jesus Christ, have mercy on me!" Regulate your breathing also, because rhythmic breathing can disperse distracting thoughts. When you are aware of thoughts, do not pay attention to them regardless of whether they are good or not. With your mind enter the heart and call on the Lord Jesus often and patiently and in this way you will soon overwhelm and destroy these thoughts through God's name. St. John Climacus says that with the name of Jesus you can destroy the enemy, for a more powerful weapon does not exist either in heaven or on earth.

When the mind becomes exhausted by such effort and the

body and heart is weak from frequent calling on the Lord
Jesus, you can stand and sing or you can think about some
passage from Scripture or about death, or you can read, do
manual work, or do some other thing.

When you take upon yourself this activity of prayer, then
you should read only those books which contain teachings
about interior life, about temperance and prayer, namely the
works of John Climacus, Isaac of Syria, the ascetical books of
Maxim the Confessor, Simeon the New Theologian, Hesychius, Philotheus of Sinai, and other similar writings. Leave
the writings about other matters for a while, not because they
are not good but because they are not appropriate to study
when you aspire to keep your mind on prayer. Read only a
little but deeply and try to assimilate what you read.

Do not abandon prayer books. Some people hold on to
many methods of prayer found in prayer books while others
give up prayer books completely and concentrate only on
mental prayer. You should take the middle road: Do not say
many prayers because you will be exhausted; but do not give
them up altogether because of infirmity and weakness. If you
see that the prayer is active in you and its movement does not
cease in your heart, do not leave it and take a prayer book.
This would be the same as if you left God in the depths of
your heart and then tried to converse with him from the outside. For those who do not yet have self-activating prayer it is
necessary to say many words, even without measure, in order
to be in this prayerful atmosphere unceasingly until such an
intense prayerful effort inflames the heart and begins self-activating prayer. He who finally tastes this sweetness should
then shorten his active prayer and concentrate more on mental prayer as the Fathers suggest. When you become interiorly weak, it is necessary to pray actively or to read the
writings of the Fathers. Oars are not necessary when the
winds keep the boat in full sail; they are needed when the
wind subsides and leaves the boat.

A spirit of contrition is a great weapon against the enemy
so that one does not give in to conceit because of the
consolations received in prayer. He who guards the spirit of

contrition avoids all manner of difficulties. Real and not imagined interior prayer is that in which the warmth from the prayer of Jesus comes, brings fire to the sphere of the heart, and burns the passions like weeds. It consoles the soul with joy and peace and comes not from the left or from the right or from on high but proceeds from the heart as the source of living water of the life-giving Spirit. Aspire to keep this Spirit in your heart by always guarding the mind from images. When united to the Spirit do not be afraid of anything, because He who said, "Courage, it is I, do not be afraid," is Himself with you.

Nicephorus the Solitary

You who wish to perceive the heavenly fire sensibly in your heart and to know by experience that the kingdom of heaven is within you, come and I will tell you about the science of heavenly life, or better about the art which can lead him who practices it, without labor and sweat, into the refuge of passionlessness. Through our fall we entered into it; now let us return to ourselves by renouncing our passions. We cannot be reconciled with God and be intimate with Him if we will not first return to ourselves and enter into the depths of ourselves. Only the interior life is a truly Christian life. All the Fathers give witness to this.

Once a brother asked Abbot Agathon what is more important—physical work or guarding of the heart. The wise man replied that man is similar to a tree: the physical work can be compared to the leaves and guarding of the heart to the fruit. Therefore, according to Scripture, every tree which does not produce good fruit is to be cut down and thrown into the fire (Matt. 3:10). So it is evident that you ought to turn your attention on the fruit, that is the guarding of the heart. However, we need also the adornment of the leaves or physical work.

St. John Climacus says, "Close the door of your cell to your body, the door of your lips to conversation, and the inner door of your soul to evil spirits. Sitting on high—that

is, having attained attention in the heart—observe, if you are
tempted, what kind and how many robbers come in order to
enter into the garden of your heart and steal grapes. When
the guard gets tired, he gets up to pray, then again sits down
and with renewed courage begins again the attention of the
heart and prayer.

St. Macarius the Great teaches that the most important
work of the ascetic is to enter one's heart and to war against
Satan and guard against his evil thoughts.

St. Isaac of Syria writes, "Endeavor to enter into your
inner treasure house and you will see a heavenly treasure.
The ladder leading into the kingdom of heaven is hidden
within you, in your heart. And so purify yourself from sin
and enter your heart; there you will find the rungs of the ladder by which you can climb to the heights."

And St. John Carpathos says, "Much labor and effort is
needed in prayer in order to acquire a peaceful state of the
mind and thoughts, that other heaven of the heart where
Christ lives. As the Apostle Paul says, 'Do you acknowledge
that Jesus Christ is really in you?' (2 Cor. 13:5)."

St. Simeon the New Theologian has this to say: "From the
time when man was banished from paradise and alienated
himself from God, Satan and his angels received freedom to
tempt man night and day. There is no other way for the
mind to free itself from this than by constant remembrance
of God. He who walks in the presence of God is
strengthened in mental silence and the guarding of the
heart." All the holy Fathers teach this. This, the greatest of
all activities can be learned through study. Few receive this
gift directly from God because of the fervor of their faith.
Therefore it is necessary to look for a director who knows this
activity. But if there is no such director, then call on God for
help with a contrite and humble heart and do what I will tell
you.

You know that breathing brings air into the heart. And so
sit quietly and take your mind and lead it by the path of
breathing into the very heart and hold it there; do not give it
freedom to escape as it would wish to. While holding it there

do not leave your mind idle but give it the following holy words to say: "Lord Jesus Christ, Son of God, have mercy on me!" And let the mind repeat them day and night. Try to get accustomed to this inner dwelling with the assigned prayer and do not allow your mind to leave the heart too soon, because at the beginning it will get very tired and lonely in such interior confinement. Then when it gets used to it, the mind will be happy and joyful to be there and it will want of itself to stay there. Just as a man who returns home from a foreign country is beside himself with joy at seeing his wife and children, in like manner the mind, when it is united with the heart, is full of unspeakable joy and delight.

When you are successful in entering the heart by this means which I have shown you, give thanks to God and continue with this activity unceasingly, for it will teach you what you cannot learn in any other way. If, however, after trying hard you do not succeed in entering the realm of the heart by this means which I have described, then do what I will now suggest and with God's help you will find what you seek. You know that man communicates with himself interiorly in the breast. When the lips are silent we converse with ourselves, we pray, recite psalms, and lead different forms of conversation with ourselves. You can control this inner talking and instruct your mind to banish every thought and say, "Lord Jesus Christ, Son of God, have mercy on me." Force yourself to repeat this cry constantly. Patiently continue with this activity for some time, and a way to the heart will be opened for you without any doubt. We have learned this by experience.

If you do this with great desire and attention, the entrance into the heart will bring about a host of virtues: love, joy, peace, long-suffering, humility, and others.

Callistus and Ignatius

Fervor and zeal to live according to Christ's commandments and to show forth that perfection which we received in baptism are the beginning of spiritual life. "You must give up your old way of life; you must put aside your old self, which gets corrupted by following illusory desires. Your mind must be renewed by a spiritual revolution so that you can put on the new self that has been created in God's way, in the goodness and holiness of the truth" (Eph. 4:22–24). This holiness and truth in us is the Lord Jesus Christ; as St. Paul tells us, "I must go through the pain of giving birth to you all over again, until Christ is formed in you" (Gal. 4:19).

St. John Chrysostom says that when we were baptized, our soul became brighter than the sun, for we were purified by the Holy Spirit. As polished silver illumined by the rays of the sun radiates light, so the soul purified in baptism receives the rays of glory from the Spirit and reflects this glory. But alas! this unspeakable and awesome glory is in us only one or two days and then we extinguish it by flooding it in a storm of earthly cares and passions.

In the divine womb, that is in the holy font, we received God's holy grace. And if we cover it in the darkness of earthly cares and passions, then we can get it back by repentance and by keeping God's commandments and can again see its supernatural brightness. This grace is manifested to the measure of each man's zeal and living faith, but especially through the intercession of our Lord Jesus Christ. St. Mark says that Christ gave to the baptized the grace of the Holy Spirit, which needs no supplement from us; it simply reveals itself in us and becomes visible according to the measure of our keeping of the commandments and until we reach the fullness of Christ.

As has been said, the principle and the root of all spiritual activity is to live according to the commandments of the Lord, and the end and fruit of this is to recapture the grace of the Holy Spirit which was given to us in baptism but which is buried under passions. Therefore it behooves us to try with zeal to keep the commandments so that God's grace can again shine brightly in us. John, the beloved disciple of the Lord, says, "Whoever keeps his commandments lives in God and God lives in him" (1 John 3:24). And the Lord Himself teaches, "If anyone loves me he will keep my word, and my Father will love him, and we shall come to him and make our home with him" (John 14:23).

Without the help of Jesus Christ it is impossible for us to fulfill the commandments perfectly, for He Himself says, "Cut off from me you can do nothing" (John 15:5). And St. Peter said, "Of all the names in the world given to men, this is the only one by which we can be saved" (Acts 4:12). He is for us the Way, the Truth, and the Life. Therefore, filled with the Holy Spirit, our glorious teachers and guides wisely tell us to give prayer to Jesus the first place in our lives, with great trust to ask Him for grace by calling on His name constantly, and to stay united with Him whether we eat or drink, sleep or are awake. Because away from Him things will go wrong for us, but united to Him all good will come to us. "Whoever remains in me, with me in him, bears fruit in plenty" (John 15:5).

And so, aware of our weakness and placing all our trust in the Lord, we should love His commandments more than life and direct all our attention to acquiring the habit of ceaseless calling on the name of the Lord. This activity will dispel all evil and bring all good. In order to accomplish this the holy Fathers recommend one special activity, which they call an art and even the art of arts. We present here the natural method of Nicephorus of entering the heart by means of breathing which contributes toward the concentration of thoughts. These are his instructions: "Sitting down in a quiet place take your mind and lead it into the heart by the path of breathing and, keeping it there attentively, say without ceasing, 'Lord Jesus Christ, have mercy on me!' Do this until the activity in the heart becomes natural and ceaseless."

This is what all the Fathers taught. John Chrysostom says, "I entreat you, brother, never to stop reciting this prayer." And in another place he says that everyone should say the Prayer no matter what he is doing; whether he eats, drinks, sits, serves, or travels, he should not cease reciting the Prayer, and the name of the Lord Jesus Christ will descend into the depths of the heart, will subdue the pernicious serpent, and will regenerate and save the soul. Abide in unceasing calling of the name Lord Jesus so that the heart can absorb the Lord and the Lord the heart and the two become one. And, also, do not separate your heart from God but always guard in it the memory of our Lord Jesus Christ, until the name of the Lord is rooted in the depths of the heart and you do not think of anything else, so that Christ will be exalted in you. St. John Climacus says, "May the memory of Jesus be united with your breathing." And St. Hesychius writes, "If you wish to cover with confusion distracting thoughts and to guard your heart, let the Jesus Prayer be attuned to your breathing and in a few days you will see your desire accomplished."

If we train the mind to descend into the heart with the breath, we will note that the mind will concentrate only on calling on our Lord Jesus Christ. However, when it leaves the heart and gives itself to external occupations, the mind will become divided and distracted. Therefore, to safeguard the singleness of purpose, the experienced Fathers suggest that the beginner should sit in a quiet and dimly lit room for this exercise, since seeing external objects is distracting, whereas in a quiet and dimly lit place the mind becomes still and collected within itself. As St. Basil says, "A mind which is not distracted and dispersed through the senses returns to itself."

Note carefully, however, that the essence of this achievement consists in an earnest and undistracted calling on our Lord Jesus Christ and not merely on the descent into the heart by way of breathing and sitting in a secluded and dimly lit place. The holy Fathers set forth these and similar suggestions as aids to recollection. From the habit of being recollected and attentive is born the habit of pure prayer of the mind and heart.

All these suitable conditions are described in detail and are considered necessary until pure and continuous prayer is achieved in the heart. When in God's good time and with the grace of our Lord Jesus Christ you attain this form of prayer and are united with the Lord, then you can disregard all those helpful conditions.

And so, if in reality you wish to be made worthy of the life of Jesus Christ, strive to attain this that at all times and in every place and every activity you pray purely and earnestly to the Lord in your heart so that by this means you may grow into spiritual manhood, "until we become the perfect Man, fully mature with the fullness of Christ himself" (Eph. 4:13). And do not forget, when pure prayer is active in you, that you do not under any circumstances allow your rules on prayer to interfere with this. If day or night the Lord makes you worthy to experience pure and undistracted prayer, then disregard your rules and with all your strength attach yourself to the Lord God, and He will enlighten your heart in your spiritual activity.

When you will be worthy of the gift of ceaseless prayer in the heart, then, according to Isaac of Syria, you will have reached the summit of all virtues and become a dwelling place of the Holy Spirit; then the prayer will not cease, whether you sit, walk, eat, drink, or do anything else. Even in deep sleep prayer will be active in you without any effort, for even when it is externally silent, it continues secretly to act within.

Hesychius of Jerusalem

Recollection is freedom from all thoughts and continuous silence of the heart. It constantly breathes in Christ Jesus, Son of God, and Him alone. With Him it bravely fights against enemies and confesses to Him who has the power to forgive sins.

Recollection is a firm control of the mind which is posted at the door of the heart so that it sees the robbers, the alien thoughts, as they come and hears what these enemies say and do; how the demons present images as they try to seduce the mind by fantasy. If this work is done with a loving effort, it will teach us the art of mental war.

The first method of recollection is to watch the imagination or suggestion closely. The second is always to keep the heart deeply silent, to still all thoughts and pray. The third is to call humbly and ceaselessly on our Lord Jesus Christ for help. The fourth is to keep death constantly before one's eyes. And the fifth and best is to look only to heaven, disregarding everything earthly.

He who struggles inwardly must constantly practice these four acts: humility, strict recollection, resistance to thoughts, and prayer. Humility because, since the struggle is against proud demons, man is in constant need of help from Christ, who hates the proud. Recollection in order to keep the heart free from all thoughts, even the seemingly good. Resistance so that, when he distinguishes clearly who it is that comes to him, he may at once with firmness repel the evil one; as it is said: "I can find an answer to the insults, since I rely on your word" (Ps. 119:42). Prayer so that after resistance he may immediately cry from the depths of his heart to Christ with unutterable groaning. Then he that struggles will see how the enemy is confused in his images by the holy name of Jesus, just as dust is scattered by the wind or smoke is blown away.

He who has no prayer that is free from distractions has no weapon for battle; this is the prayer which is continuously active in the innermost places of the soul, the calling on the name of our Lord Jesus Christ, who flogs and scorches the invisible enemy.

With a keen and intense gaze of the mind you should look within in order to see those who enter; and when you see them, you should at once crush the head of the snake by resistance, and if you call on Christ, you will experience divine intercession.

If in the spirit of humility and remembrance of death you reproach yourself, resist distracting thoughts, and remain in your heart constantly calling on Jesus Christ and if you persevere on this narrow but sweet path of the mind, you will reach a state of contemplation and will be enlightened about the deep mysteries of Christ, "until you really know God's secret in which all the jewels of wisdom and knowledge are hidden" (Col. 2:3). For through Jesus you will also receive the Holy Spirit, who will enable you to see the glory of the Lord with an unveiled face (2 Cor. 3:18).

"Your enemy the devil is prowling round like a roaring lion, looking for someone to eat" (1 Pet. 5:8). Therefore, be vigilant and attentive, resist distracting thoughts, and be faithful in your prayer to Christ Jesus, our God. For no one can help you more than Jesus our Lord and God, who knows all the cunning tricks and snares of the devil.

As salt enhances the taste of bread and all food, and even preserves meat from decaying, so you should resolve to guard the inner savor of the mind and the wonderful activity in the heart, for it will bring divine sweetness to both the inner and the outer man, drive away wicked thoughts, and preserve you continually in what is good.

The fervor of your prayer will be determined by the recollection of your mind. And to the degree that you are careless in recollecting your mind, to that same degree you will be alienated from Jesus. And as perfect recollection brightly illumines the mind, so lack of it and of fervent calling on Jesus makes it completely dark.

Unceasing and fervent calling on Jesus, full of sweetness and joy, brings a delightful stillness to the heart. But it is only Jesus Christ, the Son of God and author of all good, who can purify the heart perfectly, for He says, "I it was who roused him to victory, I leveled the way for him" (Is. 45:13).

A heavenly state will be born in our mind if we do not neglect ceaseless prayer and continual recollection as a necessary condition but remember to call on our Lord Jesus Christ. And indeed this is how we should always be calling upon Jesus Christ our Lord; with a burning heart we should cry to Him to be made worthy to taste the sweetness of His name. For frequent practice is the mother of a habit both in virtue and in vice, and a habit becomes second nature. When the mind attains such a state, it seeks its enemies of its own accord, as a hound seeks a hare in a thicket. But whereas the hound seeks its prey to devour it, the mind tries to strike it down and drive it away.

David, who was both wise and experienced in deeds, said to the Lord, "My Strength, I look to you" (Ps. 59:9). Thus it is that the Lord's strength preserves in us that silence of heart and mind from which all virtues proceed. The Lord gives us the commandments, and if we constantly call on Him, He protects us from negligence and forgetfulness, which are as destructive of our peace of heart as water is of fire. Therefore, do not allow negligence to overtake you but destroy your enemies with the name of Jesus. Let His sweet name be joined to your breath and then you will know the value of silence.

The most wonderful fruit of mental silence is that sinful thoughts that knock at the door of the mind, which would, if admitted, become evil deeds, are cut off by the mind and the intercession of our Lord Jesus Christ.

Once we have begun to live attentively in humility and recollection and prayer, we will make progress on our mental journey with the holy name of Jesus Christ, which will light our way like a lamp. However, if we place our trust in ourselves and our ability to be recollected, we will be quickly attacked and overcome by the enemy. Then the enemy will begin to overpower us in everything and we will find ourselves enmeshed in evil desires as in a net, or we shall be completely destroyed by the enemy since we will not have with us the victorious name of Jesus Christ. For it is only this sacred weapon, when it is constantly wielded in a heart which is free from all images, that can turn them to flight, slay and scorch them, and devour them as fire devours straw.

Philotheus of Sinai

The goal of the one who strives after righteousness, on which his mind should be firmly set, is to treasure the presence of God in his heart as a priceless pearl or some other precious jewel. He should disregard everything, even his present life, for the sake of having God in his heart.

From early morning it is necessary to guard the door of one's heart courageously and steadfastly with keen awareness of God's presence and ceaseless prayer to Jesus Christ in the soul. By this mental vigilance we should cut off the heads of our enemy and destroy the very first sign of disturbing thoughts and allow God's presence to raise us on high.

Recollection is rightly called a way, as it leads us into the kingdom within as well as to the future one. It is also called the workshop of the mind, for it perfects and transforms our mental character and destroys our passions. Recollection is also similar to a window through which God enters and manifests Himself to the mind.

Where there is humility, awareness of God's presence, recollection, and frequent prayer directed against the enemy, there is God's abode where hosts of demons fear to enter.

The first door leading into the Jerusalem of the mind or mental silence is the external silence of the lips; the second is abstinence from food, drink, and sleep; and the third door, which purifies both the body and mind, is meditation on death.

Awareness of God's presence, that is of Jesus, together with heartfelt contrition, can annihilate all the fascinating thoughts, the variety of suggestions, dreams, gloomy imaginings, and everything with which the all-destructive enemy arms himself and comes forth daringly seeking to devour our souls. When Jesus is invoked, He easily destroys all these, for there is no salvation except in Jesus Christ. The Savior Himself confirmed this when He said, "Cut off from me you can do nothing" (John 15:5).

And so every hour and every moment let us zealously guard our heart from thoughts that obscure the mirror of our soul, which should only reflect the radiant image of Jesus Christ, who is the wisdom and the power of God the Father. Let us continuously seek the kingdom within our heart and we will certainly find the seed, the pearl, and the yeast and everything else if we purify the eye of our mind; for Christ said, "The kingdom of God is within you" (Luke 17:21).

Theoleptus, Metropolitan of Philadelphia

When the sun sets night comes, and when Christ leaves the soul the darkness of passions envelops it and mental beasts come to devour it. When the sun rises beasts hide in their holes, and when Christ rises in the praying heart all desire for worldly pleasures ceases, pity for the flesh vanishes, and the mind goes forth to do its work to think of God till evening.

Put an end to conversations with the outer world until you find the place of pure prayer and the home in which Christ dwells, who enlightens and gladdens you by His knowledge and visitation.

Footsteps on the snow vanish, for they either are melted by the rays of the sun or are washed away by rains; and memories of deeds and objects of sensual pleasures are annihilated either by Christ, who shines forth in the heart through prayer, or when the rain of tears of sincere contrition comes.

Remain in the privacy of your holy dwelling place and strive from there to enter the innermost watchtower of the soul, where Christ abides, bringing you peace, joy, and untroubled stillness. These are the gifts of Christ, the inner Sun which He sends forth like rays and bestows as a reward upon a soul which welcomes Him.

In your progress of mental prayer call on the Lord constantly and never lose heart. Pray steadfastly like the importunate widow who moved the implacable judge to mercy. Then it will be obvious that you walk in the spirit and do not pay attention to the lusts of the flesh and do not interrupt the ceaseless flow of prayer by worldly thoughts but live as a temple of God in which He is praised without distraction. If you continue to practice mental prayer, then you will attain constant awareness of God's presence and the inaccessible hidden treasure of the mind. In contemplation you will see Him who is unseen; you will serve the one God and in solitude you will pour out your heart to Him.

Barsanuphius and John

When you call on God's name, you weaken your enemies. Knowing this, do not cease to call on God's name for help.

This is what prayer is, and Scripture says that we should pray constantly (1 Thess. 5:17).

Remember that God knows the hearts of men and looks into them, so call on Him in your heart. This is what is meant in Scripture; "But when you pray, go to your private room and, when you have shut your door, pray to your Father who is in that secret place" (Matt. 6:6). Let us close our lips and pray to Him in our heart, because he who closes his lips and calls on God, or prays to Him in his heart, is the one who fulfills the commandment of the Lord.

The effort of your heart should consist in this, to pray unceasingly to God. If you wish to succeed in this, then begin to strive earnestly and in hope and God will bless you with success.

Ceaseless calling on God's name is a medicine which destroys not only the passions but also their activity. As a doctor finds the right medicine or a bandage for a wound and these help though the sick man does not know how, the same is true with God, for when He is called upon, He annihilates all passions though we do not know how.

The Lord said, "Ask, and it will be given to you" (Luke 11:9). Pray to the all-good God that He send you the Holy Spirit, the Comforter, and He will teach you everything and will reveal all mysteries to you. Take Him as your leader and He will not allow deception to enter your heart; he will dispel distraction, negligence, and drowsiness in your mind. He will enlighten your eyes, strengthen your heart, and raise your mind. Cling to Him, believe in Him, and love Him.

Abba Philemon

By means of silence you can thoroughly cleanse your mind and give it constant spiritual occupation. As the eye turned on sensory objects looks closely at what it sees, so a pure mind turned toward spiritual things is uplifted by the object of its contemplation. The mind becomes perfect when it enters into the sphere of essential knowledge and is united with God. Having thus attained kingly rank, the mind is no longer poor and it is not carried away by false desires, even if all the kingdoms of the world were offered to it.

Above all strive to guard your mind and practice recollection; be patient in difficult circumstances and try at all costs to preserve the spiritual blessings which you have acquired. Be attentive and diligent and do not give in to lusts which secretly try to steal in. For although silence tames the passions of the soul, if they are allowed to flare up and become acute they can lead you into sin.

Even when satisfying your most urgent needs, do not allow your mind to be idle but compel it to continue secretly to learn and to pray. In this way you will be able to understand the depth of the divine Scripture and the power which is concealed in it.

Brief Directives for Prayer of the Heart

1. Sit or stand in a dimly lit and quiet place.
2. Recollect yourself.
3. With the help of your imagination find the place of the heart and stay there with attention.
4. Lead the mind from the head into the heart and say, "Lord Jesus Christ, have mercy on me," quietly with the lips or mentally, whichever is more convenient; say the prayer slowly and reverently.
5. As much as possible guard the attention of your mind and do not allow any thoughts to enter in.
6. Be patient and peaceful.
7. Be moderate in food, drink, and sleep.
8. Learn to love silence.
9. Read the Scriptures and the writings of the Fathers about prayer.
10. As much as possible avoid distracting occupations.

NOTES

1. Verst—a Russian measure of linear distance, equivalent to about two thirds of a mile.
2. Elder—venerable old man, saintly person; a monk.
3. *Philokalia*—a collection of writings, originally in Greek, by the Fathers of the Church from the fourth to the fifteenth century, who attained to the summit of spiritual heights.
4. Matins—liturgical morning prayer.
5. Rosary, or Jesus Beads—a hundred beads and a cross strung together and used in reciting the Jesus Prayer.
6. Kopeck—a Russian unit of monetary value equal to one hundredth of a ruble.
7. Troika—a Russian vehicle drawn by three horses abreast.
8. Church Slavonic—the Slavic language used in the Bible translation of Cyril and Methodius and later continued as the language of many of the Eastern churches.
9. Icon—a sacred picture venerated in churches and homes of Eastern Christians, showing Christ, Mary, a saint, or some other religious subject in the conventional manner of Byzantine art.
10. This is the spiritual director to whom the Pilgrim tells his life story, not the monk who taught him how to pray.
11. Afakist—a liturgical hymn of praise in honor of Christ, Mary, or the saints.
12. Yevrejnov—"the son of a Jew."
13. Poustinia—hermitage.

14. Old Believer, or Raskolnik—a dissenter from the Russian
    Orthodox Church and a member of one of the several
    groups developing from the schism of the seventeenth
    century in protest against liturgical reforms.
15. Skete—a settlement of Eastern Orthodox monks inhabit-
    ing a group of small cottages around a church and de-
    pendent upon a parent monastery.

OTHER IMAGE BOOKS

OTHER IMAGE BOOKS

DAWN WITHOUT DARKNESS – Anthony T. Padovano

DEATH BY CHOICE – Daniel C. Maguire

DESERT WISDOM – Yushi Nomura

A DOCTOR AT CALVARY – Pierre Barbet, M.D.

DOORS TO THE SACRED – Joseph Martos

EVERLASTING MAN – G. K. Chesterton

THE FREEDOM OF SEXUAL LOVE – Joseph and Lois Bird

GENESEE DIARY – Henri J. M. Nouwen

GOD LOVE YOU – Fulton J. Sheen

THE GREATEST STORY EVER TOLD – Fulton Oursler

HANDBOOK ON CRITICAL SEXUAL ISSUES – Ed. by Donald G. Mc-
Carthy and Edward J. Bayer

HE LEADETH ME – Walter J. Ciszek, S.J., with Daniel Flaherty, S.J.

THE HERMITAGE JOURNALS – John Howard Griffin

A HISTORY OF PHILOSOPHY – Frederick Copleston, S.J.
Complete and unabridged in three Image Books

Book One: Volume I – Greece and Rome
             Volume II – Medieval Philosophy (Augustine to
                 Duns Scotus)
             Volume III – Late Medieval and Renaissance Phi-
                 losophy (Ockham to Suarez)

Book Two: Volume IV – Modern Philosophy (Descartes to
                 Leibniz)
             Volume V – Modern Philosophy (The British Philoso-
                 phers Hobbes to Hume)
             Volume VI – Modern Philosophy (The French En-
                 lightenment to Kant)

Book Three: Volume VII – Modern Philosophy (Fichte to Nietzsche)
             Volume VIII – Modern Philosophy (Bentham to Russell)
             Volume IX – Modern Philosophy (Maine de Biran to
                 Sarte

A 85-2

OTHER IMAGE BOOKS

A 85-3

OTHER IMAGE BOOKS

LITTLE FLOWERS OF ST. FRANCIS – Trans. by Raphael Brown
LIVING IN HOPE – Ladislaus Boros
LONELINESS AND EVERYDAY PROBLEMS – Eugene Kennedy
LOURDES: A MODERN PILGRIMAGE – Patrick Marnham
LOVE IS A COUPLE – Fr. Chuck Gallagher
MARRIAGE IS FOR GROWNUPS – Joseph and Lois Bird
MARRYING WELL – Evelyn and James Whitehead
A MIRACLE TO PROCLAIM – Fr. Ralph A. DiOrio
MR. BLUE – Myles Connolly
MODELS OF THE CHURCH – Avery Dulles
MODELS OF JESUS – John F. O'Grady
MODERN SPIRITUAL EXERCISES – David L. Fleming, S.J.
THE MONASTIC JOURNEY – Thomas Merton
MOST OF ALL, THEY TAUGHT ME HAPPINESS – Robert Muller
MY LIFE WITH CHRIST – Anthony J. Paone, S.J.
NEW GENESIS – Robert Muller
THE NEW TESTAMENT OF THE JERUSALEM BIBLE: Reader's Edition –
    Alexander Jones, General Editor
ON BEING HUMAN – Fulton J. Sheen
ORTHODOXY – G. K. Chesterton
OUR LADY OF FATIMA – William Thomas Walsh
THE PAIN AND THE PRIVILEGE: Diary of a City Priest – Joseph
    Gallagher
THE PAIN OF BEING HUMAN – Eugene Kennedy
PATHWAYS OF SPIRITUAL LIVING – Susan Muto
PEACE OF SOUL – Fulton J. Sheen
A PLACE APART – M. Basil Pennington, O.C.S.O.
POCKET DICTIONARY OF SAINTS – John J. Delaney
THE POWER OF LOVE – Fulton J. Sheen
THE PRACTICE OF THE PRESENCE OF GOD – Trans. with an Intro. by
    John J. Delaney

A 85-4